The Cuban Chronicles

A True Tale of Rascals, Rogues, and Romance

Wanda St. Hilaire

Destinations Extraordinaire

Calgary, Alberta

Copyright © 2009 – 2011 Wanda St.Hilaire. All rights reserved.

Except in the case of brief quotations for the purpose of critical analysis or review, no part of this book may be used, reproduced, or transmitted via any means (electronic, mechanical, or otherwise) without express, written permission from the author.

Due to the dynamic nature of the Internet, the web site addresses included in this book may no longer be valid.

ISBN: 978-1-894331-12-8 (pbk)
ISBN: 978-1-894331-13-5 (Smashwords ePub)

Front Cover Photo: Beth Fladung, New York, NY
Front Cover Design: Jacquie Morris, Liverpool, Nova Scotia

Interior and Cover Layout: Ryan Fitzgerald, Calgary, Alberta
Body type set in Adobe Garamond Pro.
Headings set in and Pablo (Pablo Std).

Printed in the United States of America.

Edition: September 2011

Every journey has a destination of which the traveler is unaware.
—Martin Buber
Austrian-Israeli-Jewish Philosopher

All life on this planet has the ability to maladapt (to change and adapt in an unhealthy way) according to environment, stress, and circumstance. Entire societies may be maladaptive.

The people of the tiny, beautiful island of Cuba have had to maladapt from forty-eight years of oppression, lack, and captivity. In spite of the adversity they have faced, they are an effervescent people, and I pray for their emancipation. I fervently wish them dignity, freedom, and abundance. This book is for the people of Cuba.

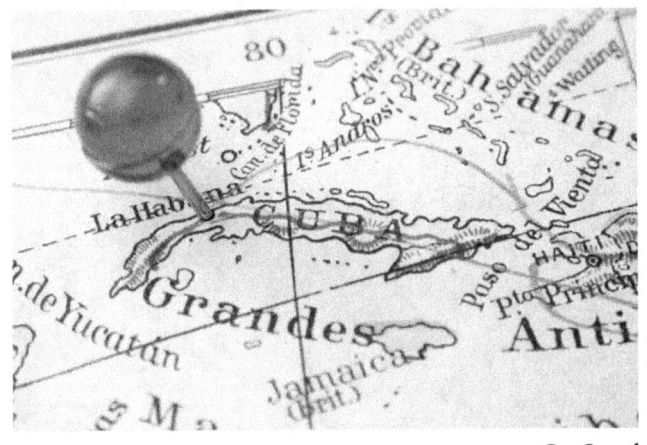

© iStockPhoto

Table of Contents

Preface: Letters to Paris ... xi

Chapter One: Beaches ... 1

Chapter Two: Havana Nights ... 23

Chapter Three: Dirty Dancing ... 37

Chapter Four: Cat on a Hot Tin Roof ... 55

Chapter Five: Some Like it Hot ... 65

Chapter Six: Durmiendo con el Enemigo ... 99

Chapter Seven: The Sound of Music ... 133

Chapter Eight: Sleepless in Havana ... 163

Chapter Nine: Back to the Future ... 189

Epilogue: One Year Later ... 199

Acknowledgements ... 205

Glossary ... 207

Letters to Paris

For fourteen years, I have had a rich, weekly correspondence with a cherished friend living in Paris. For the first eight years, we painstakingly handwrote our letters, sometimes up to thirty pages each. Writing in a journal or diary format, we have shared—without self-censorship—our thoughts, experiences, sexual ecstasies, agonies, doubts, fears, findings, failures, insights, and advice.

Oaxaca was to be the destination of my 2006 fall vacation for my twenty-third visit to my second home, Mexico. The choice was based on the wealth of history, indigenous culture, and exquisite cuisine in the region, and my intention was to have a quiet writing and learning vacation. Unfortunately, fueled by the presidential elections, the long-standing teachers' strike turned violent only a week before my flight date.

As I searched the Internet for a last-minute Plan B, I was drawn to Cuba. Quite by design, I had not been there in twenty years. Despite the urgings of friends, and my love of all things Latin, I kept my resolve, finding adventure in Portugal, England, Spain, Italy, Greece, France, and Mexico, Mexico, Mexico. Cuba fascinated me, and I would read or watch anything that popped into my field of vision about the history of this anomaly of a country, but I saw it as a dangerous place for a girl with predilections such as mine. It was largely because of my almost irresistible Cuban Richard Gere look-alike suitor on my first trip that I held my conviction for so long. Cuban men were too attractive, suave, and spicy to resist. So what is the problem, you ask? Love me for my body? No problem. Love me as an escape from Alcatraz? No thanks.

I found an offer I couldn't refuse, and so, my longstanding resolve was broken. This tale began as a typical letter to France, which I dubbed *The Cuban Chronicles*.

Each of us views the world with a unique filter created by our upbringing, our past experiences, our hurts, and our pleasures. All events and people are real—as seen from my perspective. I do not profess to be an expert on Cuba; this is one woman's journey. Names have been changed to protect the innocent, the not so innocent, and the culpable.

"Can I help you, Miss?"

"No. No. Thank you," I mumble, as tears stream down my face and pool in the V that stops at my now wet bra.

I have been sitting on my two large suitcases outside of the train station, sobbing uncontrollably. I am paralyzed by confusion in this large, foreign city. Monique was supposed to be here to meet me on my arrival, and I do not know where I am going next; she has made the arrangements for my hotel. My suitcases are preposterously large and heavy; I packed for a long stay.

I can see a phone booth across the busy street, but I cannot carry my assortment of bags and the two stupid, huge cases another step. I cannot stop crying. I am too distraught to be embarrassed. I don't even know how I got here and I am in the throes of a stage-one, code red heartbreak. I have been hit by a tidal wave of epic proportions, my entire life awash in the devastation. Torn bits and pieces of it float through my mind. The aftermath is yet to come—I cannot see ahead of this moment.

I am disoriented and dazed, as people busily pass by me speaking a language I don't understand. The occasional person glances over at my sorry display.

Where is Monique? Have I gotten off at the wrong stop? Why am I in this city? I did not plan to be here. I am supposed to be nestled in a small, quaint village, eating foreign food with my foreign lover. I am supposed to be testing domestic life with a man, cohabitating, possibly considering marriage, and becoming a landed immigrant far away from my birthplace.

I am caught up in a haze of whatever hormones flood one's body when one has been betrayed in love. I was in love—madly, deeply in love. Am I supposed to now not be in love? In the blink of an eye, am I to change the landscape of my heart and cast out this man who has pervaded my every thought since I first laid eyes upon him? What has happened? I do not understand.

I landed in this country with great trepidation; after our daily phone calls and letters mapping out our future together, his phone call the night before my departure was inconceivable.

"Don't come now. Now is not a good time," he said in a conspiratorial whisper.

My mother and father were with me in my empty, sold home, saying their tearful farewells to me after a celebratory dinner when the call came. After a lengthy discussion, with my father acting as a go-between (so that nothing would be lost in translation), the message remained the same. I took the phone from my father, mouthing words that echoed and bounced around in my head. I told my lover I had nothing left to do but get on the plane.

After a fake cheerful adieu to my friends, I got on the plane, tranquilized in an attempt to dull the pain. Would he be at the small airport when I arrived?

Yes. He was awaiting my flight with a bouquet of flowers and a strained smile. He took me to a beautiful market, one exactly as I'd imagined it would be, to purchase whatever food I liked.

"Ohhh. So this is the lovely Canadian girl you bought the flowers for. It is so nice to finally meet you," said the smiling florist.

The hardy fishwife greeted me with arms outstretched. "Ahhh. We have heard so much about you! Welcome. Do you like fish? Which of my fish would you like to take home for dinner tonight?" she asked, proudly turning the catch of the day to show its best side.

The cheese lady warmly chattered as she wrapped some fresh, homemade cheese that I could not identify.

These women knew of me? He had spoken of me? Why this, then? What had happened to change things so quickly, without warning?

I do not know how long I have been sitting on this street as I piece together the events of the past week and try to make sense of them, arranging them like a puzzle into something my mind can accept as valid. The same man who stopped earlier touches my shoulder.

"Miss," he says, in heavily accented English, an accent that I have come to adore. "You have been here for an hour like this. I cannot bear that you are still crying. I must help you. What can I do?"

I crawl out of my trance and ask if he will carry my bags to the phone booth for me. I dial the phone and Monique picks up on the first ring, anxiously awaiting my call. I have gotten off at the wrong stop. I begin to weep as I choke words out through my grief-induced hysteria, trying to speak through the lump in my throat to explain where I am....

I awaken; my moans and crying have stirred me from my sleep and I look around, bewildered. The sheets are damp and clinging to my body. Where am I? My heart pounds wildly. Gradually, I focus on the outline of palm trees outside my window in the earliest light of dawn.

Oh, yes. I am in Cuba. My heart slows its rhythm, calming itself. I arrived last night and I am alone in a charming hotel on a beach in Cuba. I breathe. Why in the hell, then, am I dreaming a 3-D, larger than life dream about Jean-François? That fiasco occurred almost ten years ago and I am in Cuba—far from the streets of Paris.

I am disturbed all day by this nightmare and a vague uneasiness grips me. I am also irritated; this is a different era and I am on a new, fresh adventure. I do not want to be dogged by an ancient heartache that should be long gone, but now hangs like a cloud over the first day of my vacation.

One
Beaches

© Wanda St.Hilaire

Three passions, simple but overwhelmingly strong,
have governed my life: the longing for love,
the search for knowledge, and the unbearable pity for the
suffering of mankind.
—Bertrand Russell
English Philosopher and Mathematician

September 4th, 2006
Varadero, Cuba

Ma Chère Monique,

After a twenty-year, self-imposed hiatus, I am here in Cuba. It is Monday and two nights have passed. I am sitting in the humid lobby bar of the Hotel Barlovento drinking an aromatic, high-test *café con leche* at 3:30 p.m., which should keep me awake all bloody night. But it tastes good.

I arrived on Saturday evening at sunset, dropped my bags in the room, and went directly to the beach. Immediately, an adorable small boy spotted me and walked up to offer berries, much to the amusement of his father.

"What are they?" I asked in Spanish.

"Grapes."

"*Gracias.*"

They weren't grapes, but I took one anyway and as his tiny brown hand touched mine, I was moved by the innocent sweetness of his gesture.

I am happy to leave work far behind. Last week, I witnessed a stomach-turning scene; my new American manager got fired while working in another country. The VP flew in from Atlanta, and the new regional manager, my sixth manager in less than four years, flew in from California to work with me. I admit he was something else, this sockless-in-his-dress-shoes, forty-six year old surfer dude; little did the VP know that each time he left us alone, Dude would start talking to me as though we were on a date, smiling ingratiatingly and touching my hand while asking personal questions. In spite of his hugely inappropriate behavior, I still felt sorry for the twit. I am no longer cut out for the corporate world and find it agonizing to spend one minute of my time talking with the suits about strategies, policies, and bullshit, or breaking in new managers, who will inevitably be fired or quit.

This morning I walked down the beach for three hours, to the point where the hotels begin. It was a gorgeous morning, with no evidence that a hurricane had hit the island less than a week ago; however, it had struck closer to Guantánamo Bay than Varadero. The ocean here is tranquil, with amazing shades of aqua and azul and fine white sand. Nothing makes my body and heart feel as contented as the lulling energy that the ocean emits. As I walked, my masculine, sharp-edged sales persona happily dissipated into the waves and my feminine, soft self emerged once again. I've missed her.

I bought a double-decker bus ticket to do an open-air tour of the area, and ten minutes later, a monsoon rain hit. The driver was kind enough to stop in front of my hotel; still, I was completely drenched. I had just showered, dressed in a pretty new skirt and done my hair perfectly. So much for that.

Ashley did not come to get me at the airport as she had promised to do. Apparently, her Cuban husband was taking her somewhere on a short, celebratory trip. Possibly, she had reconsidered her offer, assuming that as a single woman traveling alone, I would glom onto them for entertainment. I was able to get a ride from one of the tour bus operators and there was no problem with my making a last minute reservation.

On the flight, I sat next to a plain, fifty-something, pasty white man who had recently married a young *cubana* (he refused to tell me her age). He had the air of a man who had won the lottery. Knowing only too well the dating climate of Calgary, I am sure he has. His new wife is already seven months pregnant and is in the hospital, due to some minor complications. Her lifestyle will improve exponentially and he is thrilled, because she expects so little and all his actions are met with such gratitude. I give him credit for sharing his wealth; on each visit, he brings down gifts and food for the people of the town she comes from and feeds her family. As for Ashley, Maria, and Gaby, the women I told you of who recently married Cubans, I question their chances for a successful marriage once their men get settled in Canada. As an active participant in the Latin community, I have seen most Cuban-Canadian marriages end quickly. Imagine the painful shock to a Canadian woman who has spent countless dollars and enormous effort to get her new husband home, thinking the man she has found is immune to the Cuban condition and truly loves her.

I had a great sleep, my first after two weeks of insomnia. I awoke to a giant toad on my patio and wish I hadn't scared him away; I would have liked to observe him. There are lots of hummingbirds fluttering in the foliage at the hotel, and the cutest little lizards that curl their tails and run bow-legged.

The hotel is shabby-chic and quaint for a beach resort. It is occupied, mostly with Europeans and, I think, a few Cubans. I have a four-day reservation here and, after that, plan to go to Havana. My room faces the pool and a verdant garden, so it is quiet and pleasant. I haven't heard one guest speaking English so far.

So who do you think called, out of the blue, before my trip? I told him he should hang up if he was calling to announce his engagement or something like it. Thankfully, that was not the purpose of the call. It was Miguel, and he wanted to share the news that he'd gotten his degree and to thank me for the help studying. He is much more relaxed now that he has successfully reached his goal, and said that he would call on his next trip to Calgary.

It has been almost two years since I last slept with him, or anyone, for that matter—far too long for a fire sign girl. Ridiculously long. As you know, I have adamantly stayed out of his bed to avoid the aggravation of our little game, our dysfunctional dance. That said, I did something I did not expect of myself. I did not want to come to *caliente* Cuba with the air of a woman who has not been laid in two years. I called him back the next day with a proposition. Would he like to come visit me for a weekend in bed? Completely stunned, he said it was the last thing he expected from me, especially since last year during our study period, I had been unwavering. Ever the logical Spock, he asked for time to think it over. He called back the next day with "terms" he wanted me to be clear about—a strictly sexual relationship, no strings, full freedom.

"A booty call," I reiterated.

"Well, I suppose."

"Okay, but here are my terms. If we are having a sex-only relationship, let's have some serious sex; no withholding. Also, no pouting and accusations that I am using you only for sex," I said.

It is always he who confuses the issue, at one point or another, complaining that I want him only for his body and that I am too demanding sexually. If our relationship is supposed to be sex only, isn't that the whole point?

Being stranded in the Sahara so long without a lover can deflate the belief that one has a shred of appeal to the opposite sex. The morning after, he looked me over in the kitchen in my shorts.

"You are firm and smooth all over and feel good, wonderful to touch."

My massage therapist told me that too, but it is so much better to hear it from a lover. Miguel snuggled up behind me, and grabbed me for one of those tear-your-clothes-off-and-do-it-on-the-couch-floor-chair things. As hard as he has beaten the Latinismo out of himself to conform to the Canadian paradigm, he is still a Latin lover.

The weekend was an excellent prescription for a wilted ego and a touch-deprived body.

My original fall holiday plan to visit Oaxaca was, in large part, inspired by the exquisite cuisine, allegedly the finest in all of Mexico. I'd dreamed of the various, rich *mole* sauces and no matter where I've traveled in Mexico, I have always been able to find a great meal. You well know my passion for good food. I have discovered a distinct correlation: the less sex I have, the more attached I become to food. And the longer the drought, the spicier the food I crave. My beautiful French friend, Veronique, would laugh when I'd order a bowl of jalapeños with my croque-monsieur at her tiny bistro in Vallarta.

"Ahhhh, *oui*. Wanda, she is not 'aving de sex. Many peppers today. Oo la la!"

I must have been agape when I sat down to my first meal at this Cuban hotel. It was appalling. Simple food is fine, but this is mostly inedible. I went in search of a restaurant outside the hotel yesterday for breakfast and again, it was horrible. Lunch at a small, busy thatched-roof restaurant was marginally palatable. I am not sure if I want to take taxis to go to restaurants that may or may not have good food. The streets are unlit in my area, and it is extremely dark; it is not too welcoming a situation for a single woman, and few people are out in this area in low season. Tonight I have a reservation at the Mexican restaurant in the hotel. There are so many flies around most of the cold dishes on the buffet that I just cannot eat the food. I'll either lose weight from loss of appetite or gain from bulking up on the spaghetti and bread. This morning, when I tried to swallow my bland breakfast, I thought of all of my beloved savory Mexican breakfasts, with the endless variety of egg dishes and piquant salsas.

The money tourists use is called CUC (Convertible Cuban Pesos, which have no value outside of Cuba), and if you draw a Visa advance, it is converted from US dollars, not Canadian. This is a little ironic when you consider Cuba's relationship with the US and the now banned US currency. Anything that trades on the New York Stock Exchange is not accepted, so that means you can't use American Express Traveler's cheques either. I had to search the city in a mad dash for an alternative brand of traveler's cheques the day before I left, when I made that discovery. Cubans are paid in Cuban pesos (*moneda nacional*), which are approximately twenty-four times the value of the convertible peso, but we tourists are not supposed to use this currency, and it is illegal to take it out of the country.

I have tried to book a room in Havana—no easy feat. I gambled on it, and now I cannot find a computer with Internet to book it from. I tried Cubatur, the large government travel agency, but the prices were double those quoted on the Internet. The hotel clerk said there is a café on *calle* 37 with Internet, but that could be a fantasy. The woman at the tour desk at my hotel knows absolutely nothing, and spends the day staring off into space. The front desk clerk has suggested I go to Havana and find a room when I arrive, since it is low season. I don't think so. I can't see carrying my luggage from hotel to hotel through the streets of Havana in this heat.

I have been reluctant to use my laptop in the bar area. Cubans make, on average, between $10 and $30 US per month, and I feel decadent for even having a laptop. Last night, the female bartender eyed my glasses, the ones with the tiny rhinestones; she needs a pair, and her co-worker asked what they were worth, clearly hinting that I might give them to her.

I think it has stopped raining.

I am back at the bar for a drink before dinner. I remember from my last trip that the Cubans love sweet, sugary drinks, and this has not changed. I am drinking beer for now because everything is too *dulce*.

I was able to get back on the bus for the tour but, *mon Dieu*, it was boring. It goes on forever; I had no idea how far down the coastline the hotel expansion reaches. The super deluxe hotels are situated on the westernmost part of the beach. I can't quite wrap my head around this level of luxury in a country where the people serving you may not earn in two years what you pay for one night's stay. How can they not resent us? The beach in this area may be one of the most beautiful in the Caribbean.

There are many things I remember clearly about the trip with my sister, Lana, twenty years ago, but the landscape of Varadero is completely different now. There was a panoramic bar at the top of our hotel called The Sunset, where we would go each night, and I would round up playfellows. It was mostly an odd assortment of Germans I found, and one night, a hunky Italian cycling team—the highlight of the trip. I recall how we got on our flight, ready for adventure. As we settled into our seats, I began to scan the crowd in a panic. I couldn't find a single head without gray. We were vivacious twenty-somethings and our charter was filled with senior citizens. It took a little chutzpa and effort to find party mates that early into communist Cuba's tourism.

The all-inclusive factor saved us from starvation since there were only three restaurants in the town that closed just after sunset; one was a Chinese restaurant that served canned chop suey. One of the Germans and I partied into the wee hours one night. We were ravenous, and, with not a single crumb of food anywhere, we (quite stupidly, I realize in hindsight) broke into the hotel's kitchen, and made ham and cheese sandwiches.

The hotel lifeguard liked my sister and me, and took to climbing the trees each day for coconuts. He would make a manly production out of climbing the tree and the carving and cracking of the coconuts and would make us fresh rum concoctions. This task was not part of his duties, as far as I could tell. He came to the beach with us frequently, and on one occasion, as he and I frolicked in the water, he caught me by surprise, and deftly pulled down my bikini bottoms. I felt a large, hard erection trying to find a home. He damn near succeeded against my protests, as my sister dozily sun-basked, unaware. She was not much into the spirit of the sizzling sexuality of a foreign vacation, but then again, she and I have always been polar opposites in character.

At that time, secret police were planted everywhere to watch for illegal tipping and gifting, and God knows what else. The bartenders and the lifeguard gave me lessons on how to spot these shady bastards in their Starsky and Hutch leather jackets, and I became a rumrunner and buyer of contraband. I was naïvely incensed by the inequity of the system and it greatly fed my fascination with intrigue and espionage (I was probably reading a Cold War spy novel by John le Carré at the time). The tourists used a special currency that was forbidden for exchange or use by the Cubans. There were small shops open only to tourists where we could buy rum at a better price than Cubans, along with a peculiar and limited assortment of mostly Russian goods. The bartenders and their friends would place their black market money at a specified hiding spot in the hotel; I would, in turn, buy the rum and goods and place them in the same location. I was only too happy to fuck the system.

The beaches were absolutely pristine, a genuine tropical paradise. I was at my ideal, happy, want-to-take-my-clothes-off weight, and at every opportunity on the empty beaches, I would liberate my swimsuit. It pissed my sister off to no end. One day, Lana and I, thinking we were on a completely deserted stretch of beach, went into the ocean, leaving our bags (and my top) sitting on a bowed palm tree. My Spidey senses started tingling, and we caught two would-be thieves, just in the nick of time.

We took a day flight to the Garden of Eden island of Cayo Largo del Sur on a taped-together, dilapidated, Russian cargo-turned-passenger plane. It was like a scene out of a movie when we landed at a thatched-roof airport and were greeted by a Calypso band and rum Coco Locos on a dream of an island. We visited a turtle sanctuary, had a catamaran ride with a silent, sexy *cubano*, and ate a delicious lunch of lobster and fresh fruit. For years after, we laughed about the flight back. After take-off, an old woman frantically had the plane stopped when she realized she'd left her husband behind. They opened the back gate and the old man, decked out in full Hawaiian floral gear, was chasing the plane down the runway. I almost peed my pants.

The memory that has haunted us forever was the arrest we witnessed in the hotel lobby on our last day. A maid had been accused of stealing, and the police came to take her away. Her wails of anguish knotted my stomach. She kicked and screamed for her life, as four policemen each grabbed a limb and carried her off to a fate we could only guess at. I will never forget the look of terror on her face and I wanted to pummel whomever had reported her; their loss, no matter what had been taken, was infinitesimal compared to her loss. We were silent and solemn for the rest of that day.

When I get home, I must look again at my photos. There were hoards of Russian couples last time (pre-Glasnost), but I've not heard any Russian-speaking tourists on this visit so far.

My Cuban collection so far is a motley crew: the tall, reed-thin, licorice-skinned security guard in his twenties; a smiling handyman with yellow-brown teeth; a homely chocolate bartender; an attractive, fiftyish horse-cab driver, also with bad teeth; and a young, quiet bartender who looks like a '50s movie star. They are definitely an attentive and complimentary lot in this neck of the woods. The men are not as aggressive as I have heard they are in Havana—just pleasant. After I had him investigate a lurker in the hallway outside my room, the security guard offered bodyguard services day or night. I am embarrassed to say I had ratted on the electrician, but for God's sake—he was decked out in Che Guevara army fatigues, including the hat, and he said something in Spanish in a smarmy, scratchy voice that I couldn't begin to understand. He was skulking around the second floor, so I decided it was better to be safe than sorry. And I was slightly paranoid from the guidebook warnings. You'd think that as often as I've traveled alone, maintenance men wouldn't frighten me, but my numerous trips to Mexico have turned me into a born-again travel virgin. My familiarity and comfort with Mexico has weakened my gumption, and I am being a big scaredy-cat.

    I asked the buffet doorman tonight if I could take a snack to my room, obviously a radical idea. He decided to let me do it if I swore on my life to bring back the plate and cutlery immediately (as though I would want to drag these utilitarian dogs back home in my suitcase). Except for the children, pretty much everyone at this hotel smokes. A German man at the next table is blowing smoke in his daughter's face, and she is choking and sputtering, but he is unconcerned. I am wondering how blue Havana will be.

    God, it feels good to sit and "talk" to you, especially when I am so alone and cannot tell anyone my thoughts. I seem to be the only single woman in the whole of Varadero right now. Is it my imagination—or my newly acquired paranoia—that causes me to think the guests at the hotel are eyeing me with almost hostile curiosity? I get open stares on the street from the Cuban women. It could be because of the fluorescent whiteness of my skin. I have been trying to speak in Spanish, and I have been asked what language I speak; two people have asked if I am Italian. There is a cute, wrinkled old Spanish-speaking couple next to me at the lobby bar, and the man is staring at me and watching me type. I am sure he has never seen a laptop in his life.

    "*Yo soy escritora*," (I am a writer), I said, in an effort to quell his curiosity. He keeps staring.

I love traveling solo, but it sometimes poses a challenge. Although I fiercely adore my sisterhood of friends, I prefer the luxury of solitude, to closely observe what is happening around me, to listen, to learn, and to write. Traveling with a companion means one's mind and attention are occupied with their comments, concerns, and chitchat. And, of course, there's the need to compromise over where to go, what to do, and who showers first; the selfish part of me wants complete freedom. You are more likely to meet people when you are alone. Going on spontaneous dates is infinitely easier. The downside is dining in restaurants full of families and couples, and bearing the responsibility of figuring things out alone, which sometimes creates a little knot of tension in my stomach. Ever since the airport security has increased, I have felt that stripping to get through the censors and dealing with the endless hassles would be more amusing if I had a companion. There are moments of dismal loneliness. I miss the camaraderie of a partner in crime when I wish to fill someone else's head with my *own* inane chatter. But with each solo journey, I build character and reserves of power. I discover my ability to maneuver my way through the world. After speaking with many tourists over many travels, I have come to believe that the reason most people abhor solo travel is not the scariness of doing the mechanics alone. It is the scariness of what one will find within oneself in such solitude.

I couldn't find the mystery Internet café today, so I still couldn't book the hotel for Havana.

Phenomenal music emanates from every nook and cranny here. I want to dance! Cuban music stirs my body and soul. A talented troupe of synchronized swimmer/dancers in micro-skimpy suits performed the first night's entertainment. They practice outside my room and they are a pleasure to watch; their bodies are stellar, all of them. Today they practiced an African style of dance.

Wow. These are the moves I am learning in *reggaeton* class, but I am a piece of white cardboard by comparison. Two adorable small girls of maybe seven years of age were dancing *reggaeton* like pros at the pool today.

Late Evening

I didn't think anyone in the lobby would want to lather me up, so I went for that long walk today without sunscreen. I haven't burned in eons—what was I thinking in the Caribbean?

The black woman who sells used books at a small stand by the pool approached me tonight with a big smile. She wanted to know how I do my hair and I have agreed to try my iron on her hair, although I doubt that it will work. I will leave my curling iron for her if we succeed.

I can't stomach another one of these dinners. "Mexican" food? Oh, how the Mexicans would weep. I'm not sure how the cooks here make everything taste the same, with a sort of pickled pimento flavor. The older waiter was complimentary and kind.

"Come back tomorrow, no reservation needed. I find you nice man!"

Last night I awoke with terrible nightmares. I had a banging headache and was convinced I smelled gas, although I don't know what the source would be. I had an oh-my-god-I'm-all-alone-in-a-strange-country moment and couldn't get back to sleep for a long while.

The music has just stopped and the toads are croaking loudly. It sounds nice. I shall tidy my room and attempt to sleep.

September 5th

It is mid-afternoon, and I am sitting poolside and have decided to bring out my laptop. I sat at the ocean this morning under the shade of a *palapa* and discovered that catamaran sailing is included (I'm a bit of a newbie to the all-inclusive hotel; I've not been to one since my trip here twenty years ago). I went out with a quiet Cuban. He was lean, young, and sun-weathered. Aside from soaking up the beautiful shades of royal blue, aqua, and turquoise in the clear water, I couldn't help but take pleasure in stealing glances at his six-pack abs and sailor's arms.

Right now, the big news is Castro's illness and mysterious absences, so I asked if their leader is well now; apparently you are not to throw the name Fidel Castro around loosely; hence, the use of the word "leader."

"Yes," he replied.

"Good. Don't want to be in on a *revolución*."

Dead silence.

Oops.

The performers are training right now. They are art in motion. I can see how they have the bodies they have—as a result of tremendously hard work. I am awed when I see such dedication; I lack the drive for such endeavors and cannot imagine being an athlete or professional dancer.

The handyman with the bad teeth spotted me through the foliage this morning and came scurrying over, trying to pin me down for a night on the town. He excitedly ran off to get me something, and returned to present me with a small collection of seashells he'd gathered for me the day before. Sweet. I am loathe to hurt his feelings, so didn't give a definitive no. An over-tanned, skinny

Italian, who kind of looks like a piece of beef jerky, hit on me the nanosecond he spotted me at lunch. Thankfully, we couldn't communicate, and he was slightly offended when I requested that he not light up while I was eating. Now, if one of these rock hard swimming hunks made an advance….

The guests are lying out like lizards, lazily soaking up the sun. Most people come to these resorts with no agenda other than to relax, de-stress, and go back with a tan. I find myself restless in this environment. At home, the gray skies of late fall and the snow of winter bring lethargy, and I must manufacture motivation in those seasons. Sun, sand, and sea awaken my need to investigate, learn, and experience. I have no desire to sunbathe or rest. I can rest in the long, dark hours of snow hell. Living in Mexico for those four delicious winters, knowing I had months stretching ahead of me, allowed me to savor hours of meditative wave watching, reflecting over sunsets sinking into the sea, and star-gazing in my hammock. With only two weeks here, though, I have a sense of impatience to get to the energy of Havana.

I had another monumental nightmare last night, this time about work. I must be more stressed out than I realized. And I smelled sour gas at the same time, so I do think some gas source is near my room.

September 6th

I was not imagining the gas. There is a plant three kilometers away, and depending on the wind, the smell is strong here. Fortunately, the wind shifted last night.

I went on a long beach walk yesterday afternoon and then on a hunt for food. I was starving—what else is new?—and in search of a Chinese restaurant that was recommended. Need I say it was not Chinese? At least it didn't taste like pimentos. I also staked out all of the streets near *calle 37* looking for the Internet café, and it seems to be a complete figment of imagination. I did find a group of old, shriveled Cuban men playing music, offering admiring "*¡Holas!*"

On the way to my room, I got a mineral water from the bar, and a girl stopped me as though we were long lost friends. This was my first taste of the *jinetera*—the hustler. This one was a junior *jinetera*. She was sitting with a group who all had the posture and look of dancers.

"I have a CD for you to listen to, the best of all Cuban salsa."

I knew it would be a pirated CD for sale at the amazingly low price of, say, twenty dollars.

"Maybe for your age you would like the dinner music salsa I have."

Thanks. Thanks a lot.

With a look and a touch of the arm that denoted the type of sympathy reserved for a death, "Are you here alone?"

"Yes."

"*Why?*" she said this as though maybe I were a mental patient nobody would want to travel with. "Do you have children?"

"No."

Her look of pity as she asked why not made me stumble for words and forget why I had none. She wasn't listening anyway; she went on a tirade about how wonderful children are, and informed me that when she finishes her dancing career, she will have a brood of them. Sales tip number one: Making the target feel pathetic is not the ideal method of closing a sale.

I was awakened from a nap by superb live salsa music and hurried myself down to the bar. The leathery Italian was sitting with a young couple. He spotted me sitting alone, and invited me over, in spite of my attempt at invisibility. The conversation was limited, because the gorgeous, young Swiss-German was the only one who spoke broken English. I told him I am looking forward to dancing in Havana. "How can you? You have no partner."

A short, chunky Cuban woman squeezed into a too-small dress came to chat up the Italian. She introduced herself, and asked if I wanted to go salsa dancing at a club nearby. I agreed, and she took me backstage into the pungent costume room where she works. It had the distinct odor of hockey jerseys in a locker room. She chatted conspiratorially, telling me that she tends to the dancers, and that her husband left her one week ago, and her mother died not long ago. She needed a night on the town. We agreed to meet in the lobby in five minutes. Twenty-five minutes later, I found her getting drinks for herself and a male guest, nuzzling in close to him as she sat down.

"*Tranquila.* Five more minutes," she cooed. Five more Cuban minutes, I thought.

After a lengthy chat in the lobby with my friendly bodyguard, I got bored, and went back to the room to go to bed. As I suspected would happen, the phone rang relentlessly, but I was not interested in debating over whether it was too late for this white girl to go dancing.

I think I lost five pounds this morning in the quest to arrange the rest of my trip and ensure I have a place to sleep tonight, since I only booked four nights. If you want to go mid-range on a hotel, there is no such thing as winging it in this country. You can stay at *casas particulares* (like a bed and breakfast), which I do not like; I don't even like staying at my mum's. Rates are triple for a walk-in, and I had to arrange the extra night with the contracted tour company for my hotel.

When I called the tour manager he said, "Houston: we have a problem."

Not really.

"We have a bit of a problem with Havana."

"What's that?"

"Well, it seems that there is a political convention, *La Cumbre*, with one hundred and sixteen countries attending and eighty presidents arriving in Havana shortly. There are no rooms."

Say what? How is it possible that nobody knew this tiny bit of information? Not my agent in Canada, not anyone I've talked to, not my hotel, not Cubatur Travel, and not the rep from the tour company with whom I spoke only yesterday. Incredible. I raced—I had to beat the clock for the noon checkout—to the next hotel and then the next, in hope of using their Internet. No, no function. Finally, a rep at a tiny hotel was my savior. It pays to be friendly. She got on the phone to Havana and said, in Spanish, that a nice girl (I appreciated the "girl" part) really needed a room. I discovered there was an extortionate surcharge for using my Visa, so I agreed to come back with cash. I then raced back to my hotel to meet the tour manager to secure my room for that night and the latter part of the trip. I also arranged a private bus transfer for Havana. Next, I sweated my sorry ass off for twenty-five endless blocks, not spotting a taxi anywhere, to get to *el banco* for cash. With the raging humidity, my sopping white shorts were literally hanging off of me, as though I'd crapped my drawers. I'm bringing sexy back.

I asked four people where to find the Internet café, got four different addresses, tried them all, and then nearly passed out from heat exhaustion. My mum wants me to email my whereabouts so that she will know I am safe and sound; mothers don't stop worrying, no matter how old you are. I gave up and found a coco-taxi to take me back to my hotel room before dehydration set in. Now the big question: Did I actually have a reservation for a room in Havana? With *La Cumbre's* dignitaries arriving in droves, Havana could be interesting, overwhelming, or both.

The only thing I could bring myself to eat for lunch was more spaghetti, with some mystery meatballs and cucumber as my only source of nutrition. How the chef can make a red sauce that has no hint of tomato flavor, or any flavor, is beyond me. I am on the Carb-Yourself-Senseless-Diet.

I went down to the beach for another catamaran ride. On the way, Bodyguard stopped me for a chat, and his friend offered me a gift he created out of a palm leaf. My catamaran sailor was much more talkative today and I commented on it.

"Yes, but it is only my second day at this hotel. I need to be cautious."

I asked many questions about Cuban life. He's offered his sexual services for when I return. Only in the name of love, of course.

The skinny-assed Italian has latched himself onto the cute Swiss-German couple, stuck to their sides under a *palapa*. Beef jerky on a mat. I am sure they're thrilled.

My maid Annia has taken a liking to two pairs of my capris and is hinting for me to leave them. I know many tourists bring down bags of clothes and leave them for the hotel staff. I've brought down small gifts of jewelry and make-up, but my Banana Republics are far too precious and my other pair is a perfect fit, so I can't help her.

I am sweating poolside, and it's time for shower number three of the day before I go find an alternative food source.

September 7th

I am feeling very *Casablanca* right now, sitting in the humid lobby bar. Fans spin lazily as I sip my *café con leche* while awaiting my transfer to Havana. I have agreed to bring three letters back to mail in Canada for the staff at the hotel. They will write the letters while I am in Havana. Many workers have made friends with Canadians, most likely in hopes of getting help.

This morning I had breakfast next to an English couple whom I'd seen lounging around poolside, and they asked if my accent has posed a problem, thinking I'd be mistaken for a "Yank." As far as I know, nobody has thought I am an American. The couple didn't believe I wrote; they thought I only played games on my laptop. So I felt compelled to give them some of my bookmarks and postcards.

"Oh, she's pooblished!" the wife said.

They are surprised to find the high vacancy at the hotels, but Varadero fills with Canadians, and we don't typically come here in September during the sweltering hurricane season. I seldom do this myself, but I am enjoying the lack of crowds.

I went for another long walk this morning, and the beach is really amazing, postcard perfect and almost surreal. But I am being summoned.

Two
Havana Nights

© Wanda St.Hilaire

The dog that trots about finds a bone.
—Gypsy Proverb

September 8th
Havana, Cuba

Now we're talking.

I expected a bus and instead, a luxurious Peugeot came to fetch me. I give the tour manager kudos for arranging this at the nominal cost of a bus transfer. What amazing luck. My driver was a polite, quiet, young Nicolas Cage look-alike. He played spicy *reggaeton* music and offered to stop at any points of interest.

Nobody, not even friends who have been here, mentioned that Old Havana is closed to traffic and that one would need to drag suitcases down the streets, lost in a maze, to find a hotel on arrival. I consider this an important point when one arrives alone and feels disoriented in a hot, huge, bustling city. Fortunately, my driver convinced a guard to let us park inside the zone and then helped me with my luggage. There is no vehicular traffic in front of my hotel, so I can only hope Armando is as brilliant for the ride back.

I laughed out loud when I saw my room; in light of the complications with *La Cumbre*, I'd asked God if he had a little spare time to find me a room. He definitely has a sense of humor. The hotel is small and boutique style, and designed like an old monastery. All employees are dressed like monks, including the maids. My room looks pious and antiquated, and is comfortable and clean. Even the room key is attached to an authentic antique key. Gorgeous trellises of vines hang down in the center of the hallway and there are large wooden shutters with an open window to the street. The pretty little lobby bar has a large religious mural and hosts a group playing soft, meditative music at different times of the day. The hotel is located in the heart of the action, and a decent breakfast is included at a café down the street. Do you remember when, on my trip to San Miguel de Allende, I stayed at Posada de las Monjas—House of the Nuns? Their spirits cast a stern eye over me on that trip. On this trip, I am surrounding by watchful "monks," but I have no intention of letting them keep me from lusty adventures the way the ghosts of the nuns did.

In the first moments I arrived, the clammy heat and the antiquity overwhelmed me. I soon gathered my bearings and went out to investigate. Within the first half hour, I met an older Spaniard at a museum, and we took the tour together. He is a pleasant man, conservative, but with a mischievous sparkle in his eyes. He asked to accompany me around Havana. (I caught him filming me at the museum, but didn't let on.) He lives close to Nerja, which was my favorite place in Spain. It was the city where my new husband and I stayed at the beginning and end of our extended honeymoon. I cried by the sea because we had to go home, leaving the "Balcony of Europe," as it was called.

Gabriel (the Spaniard) and I went for a *mojito* at the Hotel Raquel, a place I had seen on the hotel's map and had found just before meeting him. It is a beautiful building and not much mentioned in the guidebooks. I had already agreed to come back at six to buy the smiling doorman with irresistible dimples a *mojito*, and Gabriel graciously bought one for him. We ordered an unusual but tasty pizza. In light of the flavorless meals in Varadero, it made me very food happy.

As Gabriel escorted me back to my room, he invited me to dinner at the Hotel Nacional. This is the one of the most opulent, historic hotels in all of the country and I wanted to see it, so I was thrilled to be asked out there on my first night. I asked a "monk" if it was safe to wander out of Habana Vieja late at night, and she pulled me out into the street, pointing to the cameras that were planted up high on every street corner.

Note to self: Don't pick wedged thong out of bum on empty streets.

I took yet another cold shower, dressed in a pretty skirt, and then took a taxi to meet Gabriel. We toured the hotel and grounds, and chose the outdoor café for our dinner. Señor Gabriel was oh, so complimentary. I enjoyed being appreciated once again; it happens so rarely in my own country.

"You are exceptionally happy and act more like a sunny Andalucían than what I imagined of a Canadian. I am sorry to meet you on the last day of my trip."

Am I as happy as a sunny Andalucían? While traveling, quite likely.

Clutching my hand, he walked me around the hotel grounds under an almost full moon, but I was uncomfortable with the intimacy of the gesture. I could not get past how he reminded me of my uncle. As you know, I am far more comfortable in the company of younger men. Although they probably make better partners, I can't see past the paternal mannerisms many older men display.

Back in Old Havana, we found an outdoor bar with fantastic music in a pretty square near my hotel. Wonderful bands play in every little corner and beautiful rhythms escape bars along the streets. The "MTV" music here is excellent as well.

Gabriel was intent on selling me on his second apartment on the ocean, and suggested many times that my next vacation should be to Spain. This conversation took place all in Spanish; he spoke not a word of English. Trying to understand him was taxing, but I got the gist of the conversation. He had been propositioned daily by many young Cuban women and found it sad, especially with a twenty-seven year old daughter back home; he couldn't imagine her having to prostitute herself to old, foreign men. He asked about the book I was working on, and I tried to tell him *en español* about my French love story. His eyes lit up.

"Maybe you will write a story about meeting me in Cuba and your trip to *España!*"

I found a Spanish angel for my first Havana night.

I'd read of the terrace on top of the "Hemingway" hotel, the Ambos Mundos (Both Worlds), so I came up here with my laptop. How inspiring to be writing where the man lived and wrote *For Whom the Bell Tolls*. It was perfect until a tour group arrived.

Yesterday, Gabriel and I popped into El Floridita bar, where Hemingway also used to drink, but it was too crowded, so we left. I remember well the statue of Hemingway at the end of the bar and have a picture of it somewhere. I shall take another with Papa and me as my muse photo, although my mum has, maybe wisely, suggested I give up Frida Khalo and Ernest Hemingway as muses because of their tortured, difficult lives.

There are an inordinate number of police everywhere for the political convention, so it is ultra safe in Havana at this moment. You don't mess around with Fidel's parties. I'm sure if I asked for an escort to my room at night, I could get one.

Last night in the lobby of the Hotel Nacional, I spotted a poster for a Saturday concert with the Buena Vista Social Club. Do you know of them? They are hugely popular amongst the Cubans, especially Cubans living abroad. I would love to see them. The intriguing part is that they will be playing with Los Tainos—the band managed by my once-upon-a-night Cuban lover, Alejandro. I had met him during the band's tour in Canada. I haven't felt inclined to contact him on this trip (and have lost his email address anyway), but can you imagine his surprise if he were to see me at the concert?

I found a little shop selling imported items from Bali and bought a pretty white tunic. It was newly opened and a most unusual shop for Cuba. I asked the manager how she had done this, because she wasn't a Cuban. She wouldn't say—maybe she was a mistress to someone in a high place? The locals, as well as foreigners, were fascinated and we had to line up to get in, six patrons at a time, to prevent a stampede.

It is evening, and I am sitting in the lobby bar of my hotel with Enigma type, tranquility-inducing music playing. I pet the smelly little stray housedog. They allow him to come in to rest and listen to a little meditative music each night. Thrilled to have the attention, he is dying for more petting and is baring his belly. My *mojito* is filled with fresh mint leaves, and the rum and lime taste strong and clean. I am following in the footsteps of Papa Hemingway.

I was weary after a long day of walking through the dusty streets, and watched the film *Notting Hill* on the small television. I heard what sounded like a tremendous rainstorm, but there is no window in my room. The centre of the hotel is open air, a fact I hadn't realized, and the rain was pouring down through the lush vines and into a fountain below. It thundered and deluged in a beautiful, melodious roar. I decided to take yet another shower and come down to the bar to write for a while.

Where are all the marriage proposals I hear of? Nobody paid me much mind at all today. I must have had my "don't mess with me" face on, the one with the deep forehead crevasse (which, my mother advised me in my youth, would one day become permanent if I kept scowling, and now almost is). That furrow denotes either stress or a powerful orgasm, and in this case, not the latter. There is a fine line between guarding oneself against harm and being open to new experiences when traveling alone. If you lean too far one way, you risk never meeting anyone, but lean too far the other way and you risk being a target. I was warned that as a blond alone in Italy, I would be slapped and pinched like crazy, and that didn't happen either, although the men did not disappoint in their pursuit of *amore*. It's not that I want trouble, but I am curious. A friend of Rhea's, a heavy set, rough woman of my age, travels here frequently and claims to be sleeping with and being proposed to constantly by gorgeous, young men. I was one of two foreigners I saw in the entire day of walking through Old Havana.

I did not find the bank, so have to remember not to purchase any extras until Monday.

Out of my innate curiosity, I investigated a number of hotels I'd found online and I have no doubt that divine intervention played a hand at finding my hotel. After what I've seen today, I can see that this is, for me, the best location. It is on the quietest, cleanest street in all of Old Havana.

My driver today, on a horse-driven carriage tour, was a lively, wiry fellow of about thirty who spoke no English. We stopped at the birthplace of José Marti, the Cuban writer who is revered and considered a rebel-hero-martyr, an inspiration to his country. I will look for a book of his poetry. We passed through Chinatown, which now has almost no Chinese, and he stopped along the way at a tiny florist's to buy me roses. Even though it was most likely tip-driven, the gesture was sweet.

There is a frenzy of renovation and restoration occurring right now, maybe for *La Cumbre*, but only a fraction of the necessary work will be completed if this is the goal. Old Havana is considered a World Heritage Site, and I know UNESCO is doing extensive restoration here. This is the most antiquated and run-down city I have ever seen, and I find it fascinating. There are no strip malls or McDonald's, and that makes it a unique and, to my mind, precious place on this Americanized planet. There are many beautiful, well-maintained buildings, but most of the streets and buildings are ancient and extremely deteriorated. Apparently, after heavy rains, buildings collapse with the inhabitants still inside. Almost no new housing has been built in the past half-century in Havana. It is such a stark contrast to my life in Calgary that it is distressing to think of all of these people living in such horribly decrepit conditions. Since arriving, I have been reminded in many moments each day of how blessed I am to live the way I do, and in the abundance and cleanliness that I enjoy. It seemed self-indulgent to ride around alone in the carriage, while Cubans in the large camel buses were packed like sardines in this heat.

"A free sauna," the driver said as one passed.

The dog has decided to sit with me during my writing session, but damn he stinks. He might say the same for my old walking sandals right about now.

September 9th

In past letters, I have mentioned that Alejandro has emailed me infrequently. I didn't expect to hear from him after his departure from Canada, but I thought he was exaggerating when he said that he thought of me often, but that it was difficult to email from here. As it turns out, it is no exaggeration. After many kilometers of walking, I found an exceptionally slow Internet at a hotel today for a dear price. Alejandro would have to use the public Internet houses, which are few and far between. When Gabriel and I went looking for the main one on Obispo, there was a huge queue down the street, and the house had only two old computers. *Mon Dieu.* Even if I had any patience, I would not want to consume the Cubans' precious computer time. I wonder how the girls are communicating with their new Cuban husbands. Forget about long distance calls from here. They are a ransom.

Kavel, my Indian ex-lover, had emailed to say that he called a few times from Florida and is now in Connecticut, but will call again when I return. I can rest easy now that I have let my mum know where and how I am.

The Buena Vista Social Club concert has been cancelled, allegedly due to lack of attendance. There is, however, no advertising except in the lobby of the Hotel Nacional. I could have assisted them with some marketing. I could have had that thing sold out in a half hour. So much for the chance to see Alejandro.

I am back at the terrace and enjoying a slight breeze, but still in a full body sweat as usual. Even my earlobes are sweating. I thought I had brought too many clothes, but with three changes per day, I wish I had a few more now. I got my StairMaster exercise for the day walking up to the terrace instead of taking the packed elevator. A tour group just left, and I am pleased with the sound of silence.

One of the "monks" at the hotel has been pressing me to take a tour with him, but the carriage ride yesterday was enough for me. I prefer to stumble across things of interest. Yesterday, on my own, I found more hotels to investigate, and I went to see La Bodeguita del Medio, another Hemingway haunt.

There are large groups of men dining around Havana, because of *La Cumbre*, I assume. One group just passed by, nodding their hellos. They looked much like Mexicans.

It's late night, and I'm back at the hotel's lobby bar. I am turning into a lush, having yet another *mojito*. The hotel gets a lot of attention from passersby, because of its beauty and soothing music. The little flea-biter dog is back beside me. I get itchy just looking at him, but I still love him.

After writing on the Hemingway terrace in the morning, I came back to the hotel for my second shower and clothing change of the day, then returned to the street patio at Taberna de la Muralla that Gabriel and I had found. The lunch was terrible, but the place was great. The band was on fire, and I was dying to dance; be careful what you wish for. The bandleader pulled two Latina women and me up to dance. He was surprised that I could dance, and I thought that was that. Not so. I had to participate in a *moviendo la cintura* contest, basically a shake your hips/ass thing. Cripes. I could have died; the place was packed. He had everyone cheer not just once, but three rounds, to see who was best. I could have triple died; being publicly judged has never been my idea of a good time. At least I didn't come in last. The winner was a *cubana* who has lived in the States for most of her life, and she invited me to join her table. She was visiting family, and two members were with her. A young American doctor was also with them; he'd been thrown in jail for two days on his first attempt to enter the country, because he had no dollars on him, only Dominican money and a US credit card. He was sent to the Bahamas and came back the next day with cash. Nervy guy. Mind you, his arrogance was so loud, it was no wonder he had had trouble. I was shocked when he left the waitress a one peso tip for their large bill. I'm sure that in the US, he would not embarrass himself by leaving such a pittance.

The bandleader, a happy, dark man of about forty, sent me a drink and asked me to meet him tomorrow night to go dancing. We made a tentative date, but I will decide tomorrow. Now that I think about it, there is no way an average Cuban can afford the dance club he mentioned.

Along the Malecón, I came across the large flea market. It was fortunate that I found it today, because Castro closes it tonight for one week for *La Cumbre*. I am sure the vendors are not compensated. Also, the horse buggies must stop working for one week, unless they are summoned for dignitaries. I found a tiny white dress and a small Che Guevara pendant for Carrie's baby. Last year she home-stayed a Cuban for a show he was performing in. She fell for him and made a conscious decision to get pregnant. He has not acknowledged the baby, and his wife apparently gave birth within a week of Carrie. He must have potent swimmers. I thought it appropriate to bring back something from the homeland of the baby's father.

I find it appalling that people must live under such an ossified regime. I understand that Batista allowed Cuba to be a corrupt amusement park for the American mafia—not good. But as is usually the case, the liberator himself turned corrupt; he got drunk on power; and now Cuba is a contrast between white sand and turquoise water Paradise Island and impoverished prison. How does Castro himself live? Not like his people. (Forbes Magazine estimated his net worth at a cool $900 million based on his control of state-owned companies). I am heartbroken, as well, by the animals, the many starving, hairless dogs and cats, and especially the horses. To my mind, a horse is an exquisite animal that represents freedom, strength, and pride. Some of the horses look beaten down, haggard, and exhausted, and I am told it is illegal to put them down, so the drivers literally work them to death.

The residue of *la dulce vida* that prevailed in the decades leading to the Castro catastrophe lingers in the streets of Old Havana. On their weathered faces, old men still wear the memories of what was. Easy days, rich with the flavor of *filloas*, and Havana nights, full of promise, fleetingly cross like a shadow across their eyes.

I have discovered that Cubans are not permitted to stay in hotels, so it was not Cubans (although maybe it was Cubans who now live elsewhere) who were staying at Hotel Barlovento. Can you believe it? The only exceptions made are for honeymooners and VIPs with special passes. For vacations, Cubans can stay at a *casa particular,* but not a hotel.

As I walked back to the hotel on a side street, a melody seduced me into a small bar. The lead singer grabbed me for a dance on my way from the washroom, and asked me to go out with him this evening.

"I have a boyfriend back home and I am in love."

"Who cares?"

He escorted me part way home, pitching his program, and insisting I take his number. He was enormously built and aggressive, and of no interest to me.

I bought what looked like a used edition of the *Granma*, the daily communist newspaper, from a tired old woman on the street who wore a faded and worn housedress. She was so grateful that she gave me her address and invited me to her home, giving exact directions—such happiness for so very little.

The Italian restaurant recommended in my guidebooks is in a beautiful part of Havana not far from my hotel, with a large outdoor patio on the newly cobble-stoned street. The restaurant hosts a great house band, and the meal was the best I have had so far in Cuba. Real Parmesan!

The traditional Cuban music, the warm evening air, and the good food worked their magic. Strolling back to the hotel for the night, I was finally comfortable and in my element, like my old travel self, relaxed and awed by the foreignness and adventure; How Wanda Got Her Groove Back. It was then that a handsome, warm-faced Cuban stopped me.

"Why are you alone and so pretty? How can that be?"

We had a lively chat in the middle of the street, and he told me he is a journalist (interesting if it is true). He knew of my hotel.

"It is very *romantica*."

He asked to meet me tomorrow and is to call the hotel at 9 a.m. He said that he, too, would like to go dancing tomorrow night, so we shall see what transpires.

The friendly bartender has brought a small fan to cool me, but I will still need a fourth shower of the day before bed. The humidity is unbelievable—about a gazillion percent—but let me tell you, I don't have a wrinkle on my face here. Also, my hair, which in Mexico always looks like an exploding blond dandelion, actually looks good.

Three
Dirty Dancing

© Wanda St.Hilaire

Throw your dreams into space like a kite, and you do not know what it will bring back; a new life, a new friend, a new love, a new country.
—Anais Nin
Author

September 11th

Byron, the hypnotherapist, once suggested I change my black and white view of the world to include shades of gray. It is hard to shift this perspective, because of the extremes of black or white in my experiences. The men I meet are either like Miguel and Kevin—detached, do not utter a word that is not well thought out, and hold underlying passion, but remain controlled and inhibited. The others are like Jean-François, Gabriel, and Paulo—passionate and out of control, instantly intimate, and gushing waterfalls of powerful words.

Yesterday offered me a full immersion into Cuban life, complete with a Cuban "mauling." The journalist did call and wake me at nine sharp, and immediately booked me for the day. Part one: church service. It was Sunday, after all. Paulo professes to be a staunch Catholic (of course, one can sin as long as one repents and pays a small penance in the world of Catholicism, as I well know, and his eyes spoke less than pious thoughts). It was no ordinary service; the Cardinal gave the mass, and afterward I was introduced to him. Paulo is working on a documentary of Santa Bárbara, an important deity to Cubans, and is counting on the Cardinal to approve the funding. He took me on a tour through the church, and then to the San Francisco de Asís church. I hope he wasn't trying to impress me with his religiosity, because I'm not buying it.

We toured Old Havana, and he was well versed on the intricate details of Havana's history. He told me that the cobblestone street in front of the Palacio de los Capitanes Generales is actually not stone, but wood. Allegedly, the wife of a famed captain or king asked her husband to have the stones replaced with wood, so that the horses would not disturb her sleep.

There is nothing like a private tour with a handsome Latino, complete with handholding and exclamations of "you are very pretty" between venues. It's much more entertaining than a solo day.

We sat in the lobby of the Hotel Sevilla and I asked to see a room, but it wasn't nearly as nice as mine. Paulo found this amusing and was surprised that they allowed me to do such a thing. Technically, he is not even allowed in the lobby of the hotel, and he had a story rehearsed in case he was asked for his identification. Imagine not being allowed the simple experience of sitting in a hotel lobby in your own country. His looks make it tricky to tell that he is Cuban. He said if he were black, he would immediately have been tossed out.

We walked through the backstreets of Old Havana and into rugged Central Havana and ended up in a shabby, old world *taberna* with incredibly inexpensive food. It was the first place I'd seen with prices listed both in CUC and *moneda nacional*, and there wasn't a tourist in sight in this area of the city. Casa de la Música, apparently the biggest and most popular dance house in all of Havana, has a matinée at a reduced entrance fee in the late afternoon, and we arrived for the first band of the day. They were gorgeous Cuban Backstreet Boy hunks of men who could dance like I've never seen.

Paulo danced Cuban style salsa at an easy pace, but not nearly as beautifully as some of the men in the club. Two of the really good dancers were, I'm sure, dancers for hire. They were both sharply dressed in all white and each looked every bit the gigolo. Two heavy-set white women were dancing with them, the only other foreigners in the club. They were learning and dancing timidly. I've been told that you can hire these men to dance with you and provide other services if so desired. I was glad to be with a man my age (yes, he is forty-four, not twenty-four) who does not look like a man-for-hire.

Loosely speaking, at certain angles, Paulo reminds me of a Cuban version of George Clooney. His looks are a combination of salt and pepper hair with a contrasting youthful face that I find irresistible; he has medium coffee-colored skin and is over six feet tall. Having cavorted recently with short Miguel, I find Paulo's stature heady. His style is untucked-shirt casual, but appealing, and he looks put together. Upon close inspection, his large brown eyes and the shape of his nose reveal his mixed Turkish lineage. His English is better than my Spanish, and he kindly spoke English when possible. I am having one hell of a time understanding the Cuban accent and idioms. I wish I had Anna's command of languages right now. She speaks Portuguese, Spanish, French, some Italian, and English fluently. It must make traveling that much richer.

Paulo was cloyingly affectionate and had a perpetual erection while we danced. The muggy dance floor was a gyrating, pulsing beat of raw sexuality, with hot bodies simulating the act itself, and he thoroughly enjoyed taking dancing liberties. I felt like I'd almost had sex. There were no white bread Caucasian inhibitions on this dance floor. My indoctrination runs so deep that I don't know if my body is even capable of moving like this, yet somewhere inside this white girl is a Latina waiting to be liberated. I felt claustrophobic from the intensity of his attention; this is what I meant by a Cuban "mauling," but my body had other thoughts and involuntarily responded to it. If I thought I had been sweaty before, I didn't know what sweaty meant.

The neighborhood is probably safe, but it is intimidating, so as much as I wanted to go dancing, I would not have gone alone. I was dizzy all day from the heat and, at one point, thought I was going to faint on the street on the way back to the hotel. Although it was well out of his way, Paulo escorted me. I stood up the bandleader and agreed to meet up with Paulo again at 10:30; it's not my style to leave someone in the lurch, but there is a limit to how much one can juggle men within a few days.

Paulo called when he arrived at his *casita* to make certain I had not changed my mind and "to hear your voice." He is committed to ensuring I don't lose interest. What he doesn't know is

I am already hooked; this is my favorite game and I want to play it out.

I had dinner at Al Medina, the only Arabic restaurant in Havana. It was not a true *tagine*, nor *fattoush*, and the food was over-salted in an attempt to give flavor, but it was sustenance. The waiter and manager were silent until I finished. Then the manager came to the table and leaned over, looking so deeply into my eyes that it made me blush. "I apologize, but I have to tell you that I can't believe how pretty your face is. I think you are beautiful."

No apology needed! When was the last time I heard that in Calgary, Alberta?

Paulo arrived freshly showered and looking handsome, his shirt damp from the long walk in the Havana heat. He presented me with a poem he'd just written. He was convinced that fate had played a part in our meeting, because the concert I wanted to attend was cancelled the night we met, his appointment with CNN was a no show, and he had taken an unusual route home. I think Jean-François has forever jaded the part of me that used to buy this program, although I do enjoy the thrill of the chase.

He wishes to introduce me to his sister (he has already told her about me), her husband and children, and wants to make me dinner, but I made the excuse that his house is too far. He suggested that if we fell in love, I could come to Cuba many times in the year and stay with him, as Ashley does with her new husband. I'd forgotten how hastily the Latino male speaks of love. He claims to be taken with the fact that I write and paint, feeling that would make me a good match for a journalist. I gently steered him away from this train of thought.

Castro promised his people 'bread and freedom without terror.' Paulo has a university degree and makes between $15 and $40 per month as a professional journalist and has no freedom of speech whatsoever. Journalists are frequently thrown in jail for their writing content. Ration books that are issued for food and other basic necessities, such as soap, rarely last two weeks into the month. Although extremely poor, Paulo is proud. His briefcase was filled with pictures, articles, his current projects, and his journalist's ID—the stuff of his profession and life to show me.

With our North American lives mostly devoid of sensuality and brazen passion, it is easy to see how we foreign women get swept into romance with these men. Maybe the repression and hard existence of daily life makes them so incredibly amorous; it may be all they have to give them happiness and life, and it is the one thing they can control without Big Brother's interference.

"I want to make you touch the sky," Paulo said this morning on the phone, waking me with a detailed description of how he would like to make love to me. Although his licentiousness made my mind swim with lust, I am reluctant to indulge; it seems wrong to go to his home, not just because we would be in a room next to the family, but also because he believes I am an answer to his prayers, and so might they. Can I blame him, or them, under the conditions? A man prays to his God for hope in a better life and believes that his pleas will be answered. However, I am no one's salvation—of that I am sure.

I now understand why the girls bring gifts to Cuban men. There I go again, judging someone before I have walked in her shoes. I am already thinking, how can I get him a laptop? How is a journalist to exist without a computer? He must rent time, and the cost and difficulty of the Internet is prohibitive. It was, at the same time, embarrassing and heartbreaking to watch a grown, well-educated man spend the day on a date and try his best not to need money for our activities. When he asked me if I felt we could have a relationship, I was honest. Intensely discussing this along the streets of Havana, I told him that I am uncomfortable with the financial situation of the Cuban male, that I am wary of his intentions and that I do not want to become deeply involved with a Cuban. Ever. He was, of course, offended.

"You know, words can cut like a knife," he said as he gave me a lengthy and passionate speech about his intentions, his desires, and his honor. His assessment of my character and qualities were surprisingly accurate. He eloquently told me that the women of Havana were nothing like me and how different I am in his eyes. He has a way with words, as do so many Latinos I have known.

No wonder husbands are Cuba's greatest export right now.

September 13th

I am putting out an All Points Bulletin to all women who are feeling overlooked or neglected: go to Havana.

I did no writing yesterday; my time was absorbed by *el* journalist. How many things can you do, see, feel, experience, discover in six days? After the long period of dormancy, I am awakened and feel alive once again. My fluency in fun has not forsaken me.

Tuesday I needed some distance, so spent a part of the day alone to write and shop. Along Obispo, the busiest street in Old Havana, I heard claves calling my name. I stuck my head into the door of a small bar with irresistible music, and the entire band flagged me in.

"Come! ¡Ven! ¡Ven!"

I accepted the offer and sat down, but no, "¡Ven aquí!"

They directed me to sit at the vacant front table. The brawny flautist stopped playing to dance with me, and the lead singer gave me his card and asked me to return later to talk. I was completely drunk on my one beer and happily made my way back to the hotel to shower and change to meet Paulo for our late afternoon rendezvous.

We went for a long walk, then back to the same bar for our dinner and to dance. The food was typical Cuban fare: pork, and rice and beans, which are commonly called *moros y cristianos* (Moors and Christians for black beans and rice) and *congri* (for rice served with red beans). Paulo ate voraciously. I was reminded of Marcello, the robust, sexy Italian opera singer from New York, who ate in the same manner. We later discovered that we'd both suspected (and secretly hoped) that our mutually hearty appetite for food was indicative of a similar appetite for lovemaking, and as it happened, it was. Paulo's appetite may be a sign of the same delectable pleasure or it could be, on a completely different note, due to his lack of money. I felt like a wastrel as he ate my leftovers.

I asked why, in a tropical climate where anything can grow, vegetables and fruit are so hard to come by. Apparently the government dictates what will grow and when. So, for example, tomatoes are grown only in January and February (with arbitrary changes). In contrast to most markets abroad, the little inner-city markets are sparse, with limited quantities carefully laid out.

Later we stopped at a phone booth and Paulo passed the phone to me to "present" me to his mother. What was I supposed to say? I discovered that he had called her and his daughter that morning to tell them about me. His daughter is fifteen and lives with her grandparents in Cienfuegos, where she attends high school. His mother spoke far too rapidly. When she understood my confusion, she talked slowly, loudly articulating every word, and I had to suppress a giggle. She ended the conversation with a kiss—what a culture shock.

I suggested that we take an evening stroll along the boardwalk, which was something I would probably not have done alone. The cannon was fired for its evening ceremony at the historic Fortaleza de San Carlos de la Cabaña, where Guevara set up headquarters immediately after the *Revolución*. Groups of young people, playing guitars and consuming their drinks and snacks, were scattered about like at a house party, because they had no place else to go. But the area also attracts seedier types.

Paulo questioned my icy reserve towards his advances, so, over a drink in an ambient bar on the seafront, I told him my tale of Jean-François and how this situation was more than vaguely reminiscent. I did not tell him how uncannily his mannerisms and looks reminded me of Jean-François. He quietly and intently listened, without interruption. When I was finished, he was vehement.

"He did not love you!"

Taken aback, I sputtered, "Well, yes … I think he did."

"No! He did not love you for real. If it was me, and I had de money to do as he could have, I would have flown to Mexico and shown up at de hotel. I would not have called! I would have been there to get you. This was not real love."

Okay, okay. Sad, but true.

Paulo is an interesting and intelligent conversationalist, and we talked and kissed in a park near the hotel until the wee hours. He is one spicy *cubano*, and I was deliriously, weak-in-the-knees turned on.

The poverty finally got to me on the way home, in the form of one small, lame, flea-ridden dog. He was so sweet and wanted a kind touch so badly that in spite of his condition, I had to pet him. He was thrilled to have someone pay him attention, his little ears pulled back, his tail wagging. When I turned around to see him hobbling behind me with doggy love in his eyes, I burst into tears.

"What? What *happened?*"

"I am sorry, but the poverty is getting to me."

"Yes, but this is de life in Cuba."

When we arrived at my hotel, a small, wiry Lebanese man returned at the same time. The doors and lobby windows were bolted shut, so we awakened the night "monk" to get in. We both got our keys from the desk, and I took a cool shower. The phone rang.

"You're crazy!" I said, thinking Paulo had called along his way home.

"How are you?"

"Fine," I said, wondering why his tone was off.

"I don't know what you are doing, but would you like to go for a drink?"

"Who is this?"

"I am the man from downstairs. I don't know if you still think I am crazy, and I know the monk is sleeping, but we can wake him to have a drink."

"The man I was with is my boyfriend," I said, to end the conversation. "Thank you, but no."

"But I would really love to have a drink with you. Please come."

"No, and good night!"

Yesterday Paulo came by the hotel to fetch me after breakfast. The day was marvelous, one of those wish-it-could-last-forever days. He worked to melt my icy cynicism, acting the chivalrous gentleman, a phenomenon foreign to me. We went up to the Hemingway hotel terrace for *café con leche*, so that I could finish my postcards. On the way out, I asked him to wait outside for me and I bought him two Internet cards. I discovered that I had been overcharged by three times for the card I'd earlier bought there for myself.

We stopped at La Dominica Restaurant patio last night to dance on the street where the band was playing. He looked at the restaurant in awe, saying it was the most expensive in all of Havana, not knowing I had been there the night we met. It is no hardship for me to take him there, and it is a place he most likely would never be able to go otherwise, so I have decided I will take him there as an early birthday gift. It would be the equivalent of what Kavel did for me with the gift of a whirlwind weekend in Miami. It is hard to believe, but just one dinner is more than Paulo makes in one month.

The workers in the Cohiba factory were the most destitute looking men I had ever seen. Nino requested that I bring home a box of Espléndido cigars, but I did not want to buy them in the Habano stores; they were exorbitantly priced and I was unsure if he knew the going legal rate.

The factory workers steal a box now and then and take the certificates of authenticity to seal the boxes in order to make some extra money. We went across the street to the apartment of an acquaintance of Paulo's to buy a box of black market Cohiba Espléndidos.

The stairwell of the decrepit tenement building was dark, the walls black and sooty, and when the man opened the door to his apartment I tried to hide my shock. Inside was the type of squalor I have seen only in bad movies set in the worst slums and projects. Years worth of filth layered the tiny place and the one lone, crumbling armchair had a hole in the centre almost as large as the cushion. There was nothing to indicate a woman's touch anywhere. Even deep in the barrios of Mexico, there is something far less horrid about the poverty. I have been in tiny two room houses with dirt floors, and yet they had quiet dignity in their tidiness. This was a scene of utter hopelessness and despair. This was life devoid of joy.

A small boy in a tattered and torn shirt shyly came out of the bedroom, and I fought to keep the lump in my throat down. I was sorry I had nothing but gum to give him, so I took pictures on the digital camera and showed him his image on the display to cheer his sad little face.

That bastard Castro charges $475 CUC for a box of cigars, while paying these men such a pittance that they must live like this? I can only hope that the money helped this family out a little.

I have a low threshold for witnessing suffering of any kind, be it the suffering of a human, an animal, or Mother Earth. It is a sensitivity that I find embarrassing and limiting at times, but one that I have yet to overcome. As we left the building, I burst into tears once again. Paulo told me I must stop crying, that if I were to cry for all of the poor in Cuba, he would need a bus for my tears. He told me that the people have hope that things will change with the death of Castro. Maybe not immediately, because his brother Raúl will take over, but he too is getting old and is a heavy drinker with liver ailments. Paulo said he has much hope for the future of his country. I admire such hope in the face of such adversity.

I'd read that the drivers of Cuban-only taxis could be heavily fined for driving tourists anywhere, but Paulo thought that it would not be an issue, and we walked through a poor section of Havana to find the stand for Playa Santa Maria. We found the drivers gathered in a circle, and a raucous argument ensued over which driver was next in line. It was only after the argument was settled and we were directed to a taxi that the driver informed us that he could not take me. Why argue if we cannot use the taxi? There are three types of taxis, all identifiable by their color and model. We found the next hierarchy of taxi, which is, I think, legal for tourists.

The beach is beautiful here too, just a short drive out of Havana. The young waiter at a beachside café let me use the washroom to change and agreed to watch our bags so we could swim. When I came out in my bathing suit, my hair up to keep the salt water from frazzling it, their mouths both dropped open, their eyes wide.

"*¡Qué linda!*" they said in unison, telling me how pretty I looked—in my *bathing suit*.

That was a monumental first. I love men who love real women. I am well aware of how drastically my face and body language change when I am being showered with the attention and affection of an attractive man. Paulo holds my hand constantly, and I can see he feels a sense of proud ownership in being with me.

September 14th

Paulo came to the hotel last night, and I brought my laptop down to the lobby to make him a personalized CD from my library. We could not do this in my pretty room, because it was forbidden; the desk clerk turned a blind eye to his sitting with me in the lobby, but subtly let me know she was doing me a favor. She observed us, rolling her eyes. I was sure I could read her thoughts: *This chick arrives freaked out about walking at night. I have to take her on the street to show her that there are cameras to ensure her of the safety. The first hour she's here, she finds a date with some Spaniard. Look at her now! She's picked up a Cuban and thinks she owns Havana, coming and going at all hours of the day and night!* We sat for an enjoyable hour and listened to songs on the headset, as Paulo chose what he liked.

At La Dominica, for Paulo's birthday dinner, he looked at the menu and closed it, insisting I order for him. His reaction to the peppermill had me in fits of laughter. He had never seen one. He shook it, trying to figure out how it worked, and although he did not know what was inside, he wanted whatever it was. He'd dressed in his best and smelled divine, but the fact that he had never been to a fine restaurant was obvious, and his manners were lacking.

Twice now he has said, with a look of wonder, "This is a movie."

The night air was still hot, and we danced to beautiful traditional Cuban music. A large group of foreign dignitaries filled the patio, and a gorgeous German couple who looked like the Beckhams sat next to us and asked Paulo questions about Havana.

During dinner, he pulled a small stuffed frog out of his pocket as a memento for me to take home.

The waitress made an error on the bill and added one item, and he was surprised at the speed with which I added the total and asked the waitress to fix the error. She tried a second time to give me the wrong change. by this time I was not impressed and sent her back to get the correct amount—a good way to taint a romantic interlude, but if there is one thing I abhor, it's nonsense like this on a daily basis.

On our stroll, Paulo called his mother again. He speaks with her and his daughter daily—a bit excessive in my opinion. Who is the needy one? I did not want to speak to his mother again, but he insisted, and she asked a number of questions including, when did I think I would return? She said that if I returned, it would be an answer to her son's prayers. No pressure or anything.

Later at the Taberna de la Muralla, I tried to choose an obscure table far from the band; the guy I'd stood up was playing. No luck. He spotted me and before he left, came over to say hello and apologize for the band quitting early. Paulo remarked that his manner of speech was uneducated. Even though the Cubans are all in the same shabby boat, he is still a snob about education and class levels. He was clearly jealous and wanted to show that he was the better choice.

In the square after the bar closed, we talked and kissed like teenagers with no place to go, and he played every card to convince me to go back to his place. The late night air was oppressive, and aside from the family issues, I was too bloody hot and sweaty to walk for forty-five minutes in the Havana heat.

An idea brewed in my mind, but fought against my beliefs about men and women and how things should be. He had mentioned that he would come to Varadero to see me off at the airport, and I knew it would not be an easy thing for him to do. I wanted to be sure the reign of celibacy was upended. Coming to the sexiest country in the world and not engaging in a hot Cuban dalliance seemed downright silly. I thought about going back to the resort alone, when I could be with him instead, but I knew that the only way we could be together would be for me to rent a *casa particular*.

I knew also he would have no money to go to restaurants. I remembered that you'd had that young lover in Cambodia in the same financial situation. It was far out of my comfort zone, but I kept thinking about seizing the day and about Carlos in Mexico, the rugged leader of the cavalcade I encountered on the way to Guanajuato two years ago.

He had leaned down from the horse and whispered in a bedroom voice, "Get on my horse."

"*What?*"

"Come with me. Get on my horse. Just get on and ride away with me."

I stood frozen to the spot, heart pounding, as the group waited for me at the car, wanting to be crazy wild and ride off into the hills with him and his entourage, but too afraid of what my travel companions would think of me. I still regret not having gone with him and fantasized about him long after I had arrived home.

This morning, Paulo arrived with a small bouquet of roses and a salsa CD for my departure. We visited the newly opened Chocolate Museum for a hot chocolate before I left Havana, and it reminded me of Juliette Binoche's shop in *Chocolat*. They had a rich, decadent *Azteca* hot chocolate made with chili peppers and another one with vanilla and cinnamon. I was happy to see that the prices were affordable to the Cubans. They were enjoying the handmade chocolate, a small indulgence in their hard existence.

Paulo was in a state of childlike excitement to come to Varadero and said he had not been there since many years ago, when a beloved uncle had taken him. I suggested maybe his uncle had arranged it for him; just maybe, his now-dead uncle had given me the idea. He gave me a strange look and said that he couldn't believe I would think such a thought, but that yes, maybe his uncle had intervened on our behalf.

Still not really believing the rules, I gave him the number of the tour company to call, to see if there was any possibility the he could stay at the hotel with me. A man named Roberto said that the agency did not care, but that the hotels would not permit it under any circumstances. He then asked if I was Paulo's girlfriend. Yes, he told Roberto. "You are very lucky. She is a wonderful woman." Roberto had never met me! Armando, the manager, must have told him this. Maybe that was why he had arranged a private car to Havana for a song.

The day before my departure, a message arrived that my transfer would be at the Armadores Hotel. I am surprised by the efficiency here. I have become used to the lack of it in Mexico, where maybe someone will keep their word or maybe not. Maybe you'll get a message, maybe not. Maybe the agreed-upon price of a room will be kept, and maybe you will have to renegotiate it. And time is a little more ambiguous in Mexico. I half expected that my hotel in Havana would not have my reservation on file when I arrived. Paulo carried my bags down the dusty streets and saw me off at the hotel. A small bus arrived exactly on time.

An adorable young Cuban student sat beside me, and the only other passengers were a reserved couple from England. The student spoke only Spanish, and we chatted along the way. I wrote notes during the lulls, and he strained to read what I was scribbling. On a beer and bathroom break, he asked if I knew how to dance and if I was free that night. Had I agreed, I would have really been pushing the envelope; he was maybe twenty (but oh, so pretty).

Four
Cat on a Hot Tin Roof

© Wanda St.Hilaire

Love is not the dying moan of a distant violin—it is the triumphant twang of a bedspring.
—S.J. Perelman
US Humorist

September 15th

Everyone at the Barlovento was most welcoming. I was happy to rest after all the late nights in Havana and stayed in my room after dinner. The ever-jovial chef was all smiles.

"*Mi princesa* has returned! How are you?"

Either the food has improved or my standards have dropped.

My friendly breakfast waiter seated me next to the British couple, who were curious about my trip to Havana. I told them I'd been taken out to the Hotel Nacional by a Spaniard and shown all of Havana by a Cuban journalist.

"She's been a real tart!" the woman said to her husband with a giggle.

The day was cloudless, so I found my sailor. He took me on an extra long catamaran ride and suggested I take a swim.

"It is fine if you want to take your sun in the nude."

Yes, I'm sure it is.

"So," he asked, "How was Havana?"

"Great, fantastic!"

"Have you decided to be with me now?"

"Hmmm ... actually, I met a man in Havana."

"No! No! I can't believe it! I have been waiting for your return."

He weaved a tale of love and bullshit. At this point, I was so bloody hot from all of the attention in Havana and Paulo's amorous advances, that I fantasized about ripping off my swimsuit and doing it right there on the catamaran, in the ocean, and hanging from the sails.

I took a cold shower to pull myself together until Paulo's early afternoon arrival, my body twitterpated in anticipation. He arrived an hour early and said he'd awoken at 4 a.m. to walk two hours to get to the train station and then, using the national mode of transportation, he had hitched from Matanzas to Varadero. In the daytime, he wears caps for protection from the blazing sun. There is something that so disturbs me about their frayed edges. The caps are clearly well taken care of, but so worn. I must send him caps.

He laughingly told me that if I'd taken the train with him, he might have needed to bring me to the psychiatric ward afterward (I guess my emotional outbursts have lead him to believe I couldn't handle it).

"There were chickens and porks everywhere, and you had to sit on de dirty floor. Just when you dozed off, someone would yell 'Stop!' en de middle of nowhere, and de train would let someone and a chicken or two off." He spoke effusively, his big brown eyes dancing.

He was surprised by a young, backpacking German couple on the train, who were wildly amorous in spite of the livestock. *Muy* romantic, he said.

September 18th

After Paulo's arrival, we went in search of a *casa particular* (although they are illegal in Varadero), and stopped to thank the girl who'd booked my hotel in Havana. Her colleague had a secret contact list and found us a room, after a number of lengthy calls. It was quite a distance from my hotel. When we left, Laura, the agent, smiled and complimented me and asked if I could possibly bring her one of my gift books when I returned. I promised I would.

I was not impressed with the stark little room, and Paulo could read it all over my face instantaneously.

"What happened? What are you thinking?"

A bare light bulb hung over the bed, the white walls were drab with one plastic picture of palms, and the bedding was threadbare.

I am a lover of beauty, and this was quite the opposite. I reluctantly let go of my aversion to the tasteless room; at least it was separate from the main house and offered a private bathroom. It seemed crazy to have a comfortable hotel room with full amenities and to be forbidden to bring Paulo there. And I fleetingly wondered why I would choose this over that. Then he wrapped his arms around me, kissed me, and made *picante* Cuban love to me. With that, I lost all my concerns about the room, or anything, my tension washed clean and my body chirping.

We ate at a small, thatched-roof restaurant I'd found earlier. I don't imagine there are many places you can eat for such prices while sitting on a white Caribbean beach. I know I have relentlessly complained about the food and I now realize with chagrin that many Cubans eat only once a day.

The beach at sunset was sublime, and we walked along the shoreline to my hotel to shower and change. By the time we arrived through the back entrance of the hotel, it was dark, so we snuck into my room so that he could wait for me there instead of in the lobby. We dared to sit in the shadows at the outdoor bar for the performance and have drinks. Nobody said anything to us on our way out, so I am sure they couldn't figure out where he's from.

Some Cubans appear to be affluent compared to the general populace. Paulo said the richer ones are usually the people in high government positions, the owners of the *casas particulares*, or the ones who have family in Miami. Most Cubans living in Miami send money and gifts to their families monthly, and those contributions exponentially increase the status and living standards of their relatives still living in Cuba.

En route to the *casa*, we stopped at a small outdoor bar. A pretty young girl left her group to sit with me to ask questions about the American music I was choosing at the jukebox. Paulo was hungry, yet again, and ordered a large, typical Cuban meal.

We got back to the tiny room late, and the *amor* was even better. He is a primal lover, exactly what a girl would expect, or at least hope for, from a tropically grown Latino. We listened to music from my laptop, and I set out candles; candlelight can make even the starkest room ambient. They have a superstition in Cuba: if you drink the last sip of someone's drink, you will find out their secrets. He'd asked for mine at the hotel. He noticed my playlist titled, "Music to Have Sex By."

"Ahhhh, what es this? I want to listen to this one. I think I have discovered one of your secrets already."

I am used to sleeping alone, and was constantly awakened by this large man's tossing and snoring, but my grouchiness was quickly quelled by more lovemaking upon awakening. He carries a worn picture of the Virgen de la Caridad and ritualistically kisses it each morning. Is it for show or genuine worship? Maybe it is for real; she is Cuba's patron saint and linked with struggles for freedom.

Over a bad cup of *café con leche* in the cramped kitchen the next morning, Paulo told Ricardo, our host, about our visit to the hotel.

"Are you *crazy?* Don't ever, ever do that again. I have seen Cubans thrown in jail here. Security will call the police immediately, and you will be taken to the station. Do not mess around. They are extremely serious about not allowing Cubans in hotels."

After breakfast, we spent the day investigating Varadero. A kafuffle over my small knapsack at a dingy department store embarrassed Paulo, but I had all of my documents and far too much cash in the bag to check it. I wanted only to purchase a shirt for the little boy at the old tenement building for Paulo to take back to Havana.

We visited a park Paulo had been to with his uncle as a teen. It was cooler amongst the palms at the pond with the geese, ducks and ostriches, a nice respite from the blazing sun. The house on the property is one that Batista owned and Castro took after the *Revolución*. There is allegedly an underground escape tunnel. Paulo's uncle was well placed in the government. I asked if he thought his uncle was corrupt. "Si." When I raised my eyebrows, he said with a shrug, "Es normal."

In his youth, before Glasnost, he was able to go to Russia because of his uncle's government position. Something in his demeanor tells me he was a molly-coddled child.

The late afternoon was filled with leisurely lovemaking. Basking in the afterglow, he suggested that, if I wished, he could arrange an art exhibit for my paintings at a gallery in Havana. I highly doubt my work is gallery level art at this point; maybe his brain was muddled from *faire l'amour*.

He divorced his third wife two years ago, and I found the story entertaining: She was a lawyer with a son, had worked in Argentina, had a good car—she was a successful woman. He thought she was finally the real love of his life, but noticed that things were cooling and kept asking what was wrong. One day, a friend called to meet him; he needed to discuss something with Paulo. Over drinks, his somber pal said that he was sorry, but needed to tell him something important. Paulo's wife was a lesbian. No! He couldn't believe it. Yes, the friend insisted.

"She is in love with a showgirl."

He went home to confront her and sure enough, it was true.

(Is that Barry Manilow I hear breaking into a tune? *"Her name was Lola, she was a showgirl ... hottest spot north of Havana ..."*)

He said he'd had nothing to do with women for two years. He was devastated. I doubt that the two years part is the truth, but I can imagine the bruised machismo of the *cubano*. I couldn't make this shit up if I tried.

Have you ever seen *Motorcycle Diaries?* It is based on Che Guevara's life, and I said to Paulo that surely Che would have been appalled by what Castro has done to his people. In the movie, he was depicted as a decent man who genuinely had the common man's best interest in mind. Paulo said it is a widespread belief that heroes Camilo Cienfuegos and Che Guevara were murdered conspiratorially by Castro, because they were true freedom fighters who would have interfered with his dictatorship. I can see why, everywhere you go, you see images of Che (not Castro) and can buy almost anything with his image. Paulo had never seen *Motorcycle Diaries* because it was showing in Havana for two days only. I would like to buy him the movie and hear his opinion on it.

The second night, we slowly meandered back to my hotel for a change of clothes and arrived too late to eat at a restaurant recommended by Ricardo, so ended up back at the humble little thatched-roof place for a cozy midnight dinner.

It may not be by accident, but by design that I have been single all these years. On the one hand, I was drunk with the kissing and lovemaking, but on the other, I have little tolerance for small, irritating quirks. Paulo is attractive, he is hot and intense, he is fun and likes to laugh, and he is an intelligent conversationalist. Yet our cultural differences and idiosyncrasies clashed at times. Possibly it was the excessive heat that made me quick to anger, or maybe it was the role switching that got under my skin. I was dismayed that I couldn't control myself from saying things best left unsaid. I asked him why he does not take a second job, since his work provides an up-and-down income, and suggested he would make an excellent tour guide in Havana. He agreed; however, he said there are a limited number of positions, and when they come up you must make a bribe to get the job; the highest bidder wins. If I were he, I would try to do the tour guiding independently, even though it may be illegal.

We awoke early on my last morning and went down to the beach for a playful swim. Concerns about hurricanes were unfounded, and the weather, overall, was sunny, albeit muggy. This was surprising for the rainiest month of the year. I found my breakfast waiter back at the hotel to pick up the letter he was sending to Canada. He came rushing over, with kisses for each cheek.

"How are you, *mi amor?* I have been looking for you everywhere. You are a very complicated woman!" he said as he eyed Paulo. His letter, along with the desk clerks' letters, were all left unsealed.

We had a little tiff over the taxi before I left; I am unused to men doing my bidding. I enjoy negotiating and winning, and he had not negotiated the taxi properly. He said he knew Cuba better than I, and I said I knew how to negotiate better than he. I won, as I knew I would.

En route to the airport, we met with no problems, in spite of CNN's warnings that a fleet of boats filled with Cuban-Americans in protest of *La Cumbre* were coming from Miami to the shores of Varadero at that hour. Paulo was reminded of the boatloads of Cubans fleeing to the shores of Miami and told me what life was like during the austerity period, *Período Especial*, as Castro dubbed it, when in 1990 the Soviet cut their massive subsidies. There were many shortages, and hunger was a daily certainty. Paulo remembers it as a long period of great hardship and anguish.

He was every bit the melodramatic Latino during our kiss-filled farewell over drinks at the smoky airport bar. For me, it was the bittersweet end of a heady vacation, but for him it was back to the hard reality of Cuban life in Havana.

Five
Some Like it Hot

© Wanda St.Hilaire

I wrote the story myself. It's all about a girl who lost her reputation but never missed it.
—Mae West
Actress

September 26th

Bonjour Mon Amie,

I have a couple of minutes to write and then I am off to Edmonton. I am stopping along the way for an early morning massage with Pete, Mr. Intuition. I shall see if he notices any change in my body. In the middle of my first massage, he asked why I was punishing myself by not having sex for so long; that's how obviously my body read.

Since my return from Cuba, the shift in my life and energy has created many small but good things. Life is a cycle, and this trip has created a much-needed upswing this year. The deep rut I was caught in caused me unusual trepidation, and I almost aborted my vacation due to the necessity of a last minute change in plans. The holiday was so pleasurable that I am assuming it is the universe's reward to me for crawling outside my self-created trenches, feeling the fear, and doing it anyway.

There were many messages from friends welcoming me back, and I have two clients interested in developing a friendship who'd called while I was away and were awaiting my return. Kavel had left two messages from Florida, and Miguel had called to book a rendezvous.

September 29th

As Paulo had requested, I called briefly on Sunday when I returned. He'd written a letter and was going to email it the following day, but I heard nothing, so I assumed that he was not allowed in the Ambos Mundos Hotel where I'd bought the Internet cards or the lines were down. He called collect a few times when I wasn't home, but I am not going to start a habit of accepting collect calls from Cuba.

Miguel called back to spend the weekend with me here. I am enjoying the influx of men in my life. I unplugged the phone to avert an awkward situation, should Paulo call; it would not go over well on either end. I would not answer Miguel's queries about whether I'd met someone in Cuba. I don't think it's any of his business; he set the firm no-strings agreement. Although not consciously, he was, with ardent kisses and uncommon affection, reclaiming territory he sensed had been invaded. On Monday morning, he made love to me with more than normal intensity before rising. I got up and plugged the phone in without thinking. While he was basking, I saw Paulo's number come up on the ringing screen, so did not pick up.

"Do you want to go get us a latte?" I asked Miguel.

"No, not really."

I waited a few more minutes.

"Are you going to get up and take a shower?"

"Yes … yah … mmm hmmmmmm."

More lollygagging.

He finally arose and got in the shower, so I grabbed the phone and went to the basement laundry room to return the call to Cuba. The Internet lines had been down for almost a week at Ambos Mundos. Paulo had many questions and many kisses and asked if I would return for my birthday and Christmas.

"I wish I would open my eyes in the morning and it would be December and you would already be here."

I had to race upstairs to grab a pen for his new address—Miguel was still showering—and run back downstairs to end the call. Am I turning into a man?

His subsequent email was full of love and lust and "missing you after so many beautiful moments and days." I have mailed him my book of poetry and a letter, but of course, it has not arrived and may never arrive with Cuba's mail system. I have no inclination to fall in love with him. I do, however, love the excitement of a foreign tryst and am seriously considering spending my Christmas vacation in Cuba.

I had dinner with Darshana one night after my return. I told her that I would like to help improve Paulo's life a little while I am in it and wish to bring him a used laptop. She was given her brother's laptop after his death and felt she was ready to let it go. For the cause of the Cuban condition, she is willing to offer it gratis. This alone will vastly improve his career opportunities; he'd had a meeting with the Havana paper while I was there, with the idea of doing some work on *La Cumbre*, but the editor had refused to lend him her laptop, which her children were playing games on at the time of the meeting. I have a list of gifts I want to bring and I will tell everyone at home to forgo a Christmas gift exchange with me this year. Instead, I will bring down gifts for him and his family and for children in Havana.

In response to your letter: I agree—filth and poverty have nothing to do with each other. In the case of the cigar man, I sensed a complete lack of hope. The oppression and years of destitution had caused him to give up and no longer care about his surroundings.

I am certainly the furthest thing from a political expert, but I would say you might be giving Castro a lot of benefit of the doubt. He has had an inordinate forty-six years to succeed at his plan, and the regime is failing. That said, I don't know if anything really works optimally, because it is in the nature of man to abuse power and become corrupt when in such a position, no matter what the system. Point in question: Bush. I would hate to see the US, or any country, go in once again and exploit. It would destroy the culture of the island, and it was wonderful to be in a place free of hands-on American influence. The people get information and are influenced by the many Cubans sending money and gifts from Miami, but they don't have the Americans on their soil dictating their whims. On my last trip to Mexico, I attended a Christmas soirée in a wealthy American/Canadian neighborhood and was saddened by the destruction of Mexican life. We push and demand endlessly until we get all the comforts of home, and it erodes the way of life and the uniqueness of the country. Cuba has been plundered, raped and pillaged quite enough in its illustrious life.

I attended the International Film Festival and saw a movie yesterday called *The Conquistadors of Cuba*. It is a documentary following the life of the cars of three men: Batista, Guevara, and Lansky, the famed Jewish mob boss who was giving enormous amounts of money to the Batista regime. Lansky built the Hotel Riviera and had ten opulent American cars at his and Batista's disposal. They interviewed both Lansky's driver and his chef, as well as the chef's wife. They all seemed to love this godfather, Lansky. I don't quite understand what the US's interest would be in Cuba at this point in time, except maybe for strategic homeland security hogwash.

October 2nd

If only I could hold that travel feeling and aura all the time, but it is impossible to do when living the everyday business life. It is Monday morning, a couple of reports are due and the reality of sales life has crowded out the holiday happies. The weather is dreary, and I am suffering from hormonal blues. Moroccan Boy, the young guy who has not given up since February, has been calling like crazy, but I haven't returned his calls.

October 3rd

Paulo definitely has a physical affect on me, even on the phone. We have been communicating via phone and Internet, but the connections for both are horrible. Apparently a new rule was just implemented two days ago: Cubans are no longer permitted to use the Internet in hotels. What a life. He was able to convince the manager at the Ambos Mundos to allow him in by showing his journalist's identification and by appealing to the man's sense of romance. He said he had a Canadian girlfriend, and emailing is the only way to communicate with me. Rules and laws arbitrarily change week to week.

He is set on the idea of my coming at Christmas for as long as possible. Surprisingly, Ricardo, the owner of the *casa particular* in Varadero where we stayed, had called Paulo to ask how I am—I would have thought he and his wife had dismissed me as a bitchy foreigner. I was not overly affable. Paulo wants me to go to Cienfuegos to meet his parents and daughter, so I wrote back to let him know I am *not* going anywhere to meet any family.

My own mother's reaction has surprised me. My sister suggested I use caution in telling my mum about Paulo. We expected something like, "Oh, my God. Not another foreigner! This one just wants money." *Au contraire.* Her response was, "So what if he has no money? You can build a life from scratch together. It's not like you have children to worry about."

She must *really* be desperate to marry me off.

October 4th

Lynn and I discussed Paulo and the Cuban condition yesterday. I do realize he is placing a lot of hope in me that this will turn serious and I will be the answer to a new life for him. I can sense his expectation and I must clarify that my visit is strictly for a vacation and for pleasure, nothing more.

Probably concerned, Lynn asked her mother to do some of her psychic divining and called me with the answers this morning. The results, which didn't exactly give me a warm fuzzy feeling, were:

Is Paulo looking at Wanda as a meal ticket? Yes.

Is he madly in love with her as he professes? No.

Should Wanda return to Cuba? An emphatic *No*.

I take this stuff with a grain of salt, but it casts further doubt. I must soon decide on my ticket purchase. If I stay home, I can see myself pouting in a snow bank. Christmas is the time of year when I most feel an ache in my heart and long to share the holidays with a man. The fact that I have been single and alone for such a long time becomes glaringly obvious and painful. I get claustrophobic at home during the holidays now; I am seduced by the idea of spending my birthday, Christmas, and New Year's Eve with a lover in the sunshine of Varadero and dancing to the sultry salsa of Havana.

October 5th

Two not completely intelligible love letters have arrived via email. Paulo is obviously using his English dictionary for translations. I read them to my sister.

"Who in the hell writes these kinds of letters? They read like a Harlequin Romance!"

October 8th

It's a delicious Sunday morning and I am in Edmonton in Miguel's bed. My sister and I behaved like naughty teenagers, saying that I was going to stay at a girlfriend's place since mum is in love with the idea of Paulo and frankly, it doesn't sound so good. Lana wants to meet Miguel, so suggested he come for Thanksgiving dinner today. It doesn't fit the terms of our agreement, but she has heard so much about this man for the past five years that she wants to put a face to the name. Plus, she is the family inquirer, the "Town Crier" of the clan.

Last night was wonderful. Does Miguel sense competition? He eagerly agreed to come to the family dinner. We had a leisurely morning, and he is upstairs showering right now. Our lovemaking this morning was short but sweet, and I wish I could stay here all day and all night for more. He has easily fallen back into calling me Wandita, and I confess that this diminutive version of my name feels like a caress. This is the first time I have stayed at his new home, and much to my surprise, he made tamales for breakfast and went out to get my morning latte.

I enjoy Miguel more because of Paulo. I awoke in fantastic form and was daydreaming of both men while in bed this morning with Miguel, mixing the two of them in my heart, mind, and body. My sister cannot imagine managing two men at the same time, and although doing so is still taboo, the truth of the matter is, I am enjoying it tremendously. I think Miguel enjoys me more because I am a little elusive now, because a part of me is elsewhere. For whatever reason, I awoke with joy this morning. My body is rhapsodic.

I weighed myself last week for the first time in months and I have lost ten pounds! The salsa aerobics and lovemaking have finally had an effect on my body, and the stubborn excess weight has decided to leave.

Thanksgiving Day

I was surprised that Miguel stayed with my family until midnight. If I were he, I would have been bored to death and feigned an excuse to leave. My dad watched us like a hawk, trying to figure out what is going on. I'm sure he can't quite wrap his head around the intimacy of my recent pictures with Paulo, and then Miguel's showing up for dinner. What is he to make of such a daughter?

October 12th

How corporate work cuts into real life—the good life. We've got it backwards in this society. I observe the beautiful life you and Anna have manifested without working. Most of the populace have their nine to five jobs and don't even contemplate that life can be like yours. You two live completely and freely outside the norm. It always gives me hope in my dream, that it can be done, that I will live a creative existence in the places I love. You are leaving Paris for Guadeloupe as well as Seville? I wanna be you when I grow up.

I am awaiting a reply from the travel agent. It is peak season, but what the hell? Paulo said last week that he would be happy to cook for me (better for my "economy"), either at his place or at a *casa particular*.

Miguel calls frequently and asks each time if I have a lover in Calgary, and I can honestly answer no. Cuba is a sensitive topic for him; it is odd, considering that we only started sleeping with each other one week prior to my trip.

"This is not fair. You fly off to Cuba and do God knows what and I can't have another lover." (I had agreed to his terms and never said that; I had only suggested he reserve his limited energy for me.)

If he goes away for Christmas, as he always has, he could easily take a lover in his homeland of Chile or go to see Rosa once again in Madrid.

"What do you see in me?" he asked once more. I am tempted to say, "A beautiful, hard body and a nice package," but I don't. Why ask when we are only part-time lovers?

I booked my flight early this morning and am to leave December 18th for Varadero. I called Paulo afterward to give him the news.

"Really? You really paid for it? For sure?" he yelped, thrilled with the news. He said not to book a hotel, that I must stay with him. I doubt that I will; the *casas particulares* in Havana are plentiful and inexpensive.

October 15th

I am seeing life through a pheromone-induced haze since returning to Calgary and have confessed to Anna that I can't seem to get even the simplest tasks accomplished. I only want to write, dance, eat, sleep, and make love or think about making love. I seem to fit the profile of a classic sufferer of Peter Pan Syndrome, a head in the clouds Sagittarian. Anna admitted she is the same right now since meeting her new man. Rita and her Scottish lover have rekindled their flame, and he is planning another trip to visit her. You tell me that you accepted Antoine's advances this time and had a tryst in his Parisian love nest. Even nose-to-the-grindstone Belinda, who works fourteen hours a day and never goes out, has a new lover. Methinks Venus is up to something.

The following letter arrived from Paulo and I've translated it best as I can. I have the stack of love letters and declarations from Jean-François, so I know how *that* can go, but I am basking in the eighteenth century romance of it all. It is a tall glass of water after a two-year drought.

> My Dear and Beloved Wanda,
>
> As you can see, I am writing to you in Spanish; thus, you can practice a little and I can write more quickly. You can translate with greater ease than I from English to Spanish.
>
> I count the days until your arrival, as well as the hours and the minutes. Love has arrived at my door and is staying. Time will demonstrate it and God wants it so. My beautiful and sweet princess, here we have very hot weather. I have opened another, better email account. It is important that I have found this and I will write you more often, longer letters, messages, etc. It pleases me very much that you call me every week, feeds my spirit and my love for you. My single request is your patience and that you continue calling me as until now you have done.
>
> I will not fail you, nor ever disappoint you. I am willing to devote my life to you if you wish it, to offer you all my love, and to fight for you, to live for you, to make dreams a reality and to pursue life together towards the future, which will always get better. I long to be able to watch the waves, the stars, and to feel that with you by my side the dawns are warmer and more romantic; everything is always better when I am by your side. It is those small things that fill a man with satisfaction, one who is determined to love and to give all of his soul to a beautiful woman like you, because you deserve it.

You will be my soul, you will be my angel, you will be my faith, you will be the star that illuminates the sky of my heart, you will be my water, you will be my air, you will be the calm, you will be the fire that burns in my soul. I put my heart in your hands, which I hope you value, since our lives found us on the same path.

As you will understand, my mother's health worries me much, especially with my father's absence. You know the situation, how difficult it is with the medicines, and the problem with food that strikes us constantly. You know well how things are here; it is hard, but it is reality. Once the tests are finished, I want her to come to Havana so that she is taken care of by the best specialists in the best hospital of the city. In the middle of these preoccupations, I wait for the arrival this month of the gentleman who owns the Venezuelan newspaper that I will interview with.

Aside from this, the news of your flight fills me with joy, courage to fight, patience to wait for you. I know that you are interested in knowing my life; I also want to know yours. I attach a brief curriculum vitae on my work life.

I also desire to write a book and to learn to play the saxophone, which is the most romantic instrument. I have spoken to you enough about my training, my work life, and my family.

Receive a strong hug, and thousands of kisses, from a man who wants you, desires you, and waits for you with open arms and a longing body. Continue studying Spanish, and excuse me for having written to you in Spanish. I hope you can translate with the computer.

I love you,
I want you,
Kisses....
your Paulo.
I await your call Tuesday.

As Shirley Valentine said, "Aren't men full of shit?"

October 16th

It was gray all weekend; this is the worst time of year when the snow begins and all is so stark and bleak and sad looking. For me, the joy brought by sun and summer ends, and I want to sleep, sleep, sleep. I am pleased I have a ticket to sunny Cuba.

As I suspected, my mum has been Christmas shopping for Paulo already. I gave her a project: Paulo's nephews apparently love playing pirates, and since it is Halloween season, she can find costumes. I will be loaded with goodies like Santa Claus this Christmas.

I had a dream yesterday morning that I was at a fair. A woman walked up to me and told me she was a psychic.

"Many men love you. I think you need to know that."

Maybe a little sleep fantasy? I was jolted out of the dream by the phone. My ex-husband called to say he was traveling through the city and asked if we could meet later in the day. I didn't go, and now I am truly sorry. For some reason, I think he needed to see me.

Anna helped me translate another letter from Paulo yesterday. Her new lover rolled his eyes at the poetics.

A Diana Ross song is playing here at the café. *Touch Me in the Morning*. Music is a powerful memory conduit, and I am having a flashback to my first school dance when, at only twelve years old and in seventh grade, I said yes to a dance with an older man, a mature looking ninth grader. He had something hard in his pocket and gave me my first French kiss while dancing to this song. I was stunned, scared, and excited all at once. It was then and there that everything began.

October 23rd

I spent Friday evening at home to rest and savor a book. Saturday, Miguel was to call and let me know if he could make it to town after work. He had some home renos to take care of on Sunday, so opted out of coming. I made a spur of the moment decision, got myself into my new sexy red Cuban Christmas shirt, and went alone to a wine tasting salsa party at my dance studio. It looked like it would be a bust of a party, all couples sitting quietly for the wine tasting and dinner. The band arrived, and people started filing in. It was the best party I have been to in years! There was an abundance of beautiful and friendly men to dance with, and I was on the floor all night. In the middle of the party, the fire alarms sounded and we were evacuated. It was not a drill, and flames shot up from the underground parking grate, but the firemen had it under control quickly, and the party resumed without a hitch. Even though I got home late, I was completely energized the next day.

Yesterday at the studio, I bought my first real dancing shoes, a beautiful red satin pair. I think they will be perfect for my trip.

I received an email from Havana on Friday, but this one was not from Paulo. It was from Alejandro. Remember that I was going to surprise him by showing up at their concert in Havana at the Hotel Nacional, but it was cancelled, and that is the night I met Paulo. The group will be returning to Calgary in November, and he wants to see me. I would like to see him, but I don't know if it's a good idea to take on a third lover, especially one from Havana.

October 28th

I was out last night at an amazingly boring Canadian party held at a restaurant. People milled around in hushed tones, drinks in hand, quietly nodding at each other, while indistinguishable elevator music played softly in the background. No overt glances were taken nor passes made at this little shindig. What a bleak contrast to last weekend. The freedom and standard of life in Canada are second to none—I'll never dispute it—but our culture is truly insipid. We have perpetuated a vicious cycle; women are so paranoid about perverts that we're all paralyzed. My friend Deb once told me about the high level of sexual harassment in the workplace in the '70s; it was considered to be the norm. Nobody questioned it. And I can attest that it occurred in the next generation; when I was nineteen, my rumpled, married-with-children boss literally chased me around his desk and practically assaulted me. It is absolutely appropriate that we no longer have to tolerate this kind of abuse; however, I believe we've tipped the scales too far, and now, men in Canada are afraid to be men.

A new barista, a beautiful Jamaican, started working mornings at my café. I began to await my morning latte with glee, knowing he would flirt with me—a little man-woman interaction to start my day off on a bright note. I met a friend there one morning while he was working. She came to the table with her coffee, upset with his flirtatious behavior, thinking he was a freak. She said that her friend, a twenty-something girl, refused to return to the coffee shop because of his remarks. I was astounded. He was a warm and friendly man and I took his playfulness as a treat that is hard to come by in our day-to-day lives. Men all over Europe, the Caribbean, and Latin America have women uppermost on the brain. Yet here in Canada, it seems as though the men have mostly lost their *cojónes*; we have hammered the natural instincts out of them and now they focus their sexual energy on the almighty dollar and on sports. Why do we want a society where strangers are afraid to speak to each other? I want to start a crusade: "Bring back lust. Why ration passion?"

Miguel came to my hotel one night this week in Edmonton while I was on business, but it was unsatisfying; he talked for far too long, wasting valuable recreation time. After our lovemaking, he said he should leave.

"Buh-bye," I said.

"Have your way with me, then kick me out?"

"Yup."

I couldn't get him to shut up or leave after that.

October 29th

The letters from Paulo have been sweet. He is looking for an apartment in Havana with a kitchen, so he can cook and we can have privacy. He has told his friends about me and is planning a birthday party. I sometimes feel ill about his circumstances; his contract with the Venezuelan newspaper fell through—a typical situation. He has taken what he can for work in between journalistic ventures. It is a desperate life.

I forgot the change from daylight saving to standard time this morning, and it worked out well. I can sit and have a latte at the café before salsa class. I left Miguel at home in my bed. He wants to study for yet another certification of some type.

Last night I had the apartment spotless, with twinkling candles everywhere and a beautiful dinner made. This is the same preparation I go through for any friend I entertain, be it man or woman. Miguel walked in, looked around, and stopped in his tracks.

"What the hell is this?"

He's ever suspicious that I am trying to entrap him into a serious relationship. I remember one Sunday morning a long time ago when I'd brought an enormous breakfast in bed to my younger Polish lover. I did it for myself every Sunday morning and was only doing what came naturally to me—sharing. The following week, he informed me that his friends had advised him that only a woman in love would do such a thing. He wanted to remind me that he was not interested in a serious relationship. He never got another meal in my home, but months later, pleaded that I meet with his parents who'd arrived from Poland, so that they could meet the future Mrs. Chmelovich. In his dreams.

Miguel was afraid to break the news that he is going back home to Chile for a month at Christmas, assuming I would be upset. I am secretly pleased; now I don't have to make excuses for returning to Cuba.

While he was here, I thought of what you said about the differences between France and Canada, the absurd North American standards of beauty, and how we can never meet these images of perfection. The thing I dislike most about my body is the little bulge around my waist—my nemesis. I bought my first pair of true low-rise jeans and was wearing them when Miguel arrived, in spite of the roll. He grabbed me around the waist and said, "*This is driving me crazy. I love it!*"

Who knew?

October 30th

Miguel left this morning after breakfast. We had a pleasurable yesterday hanging out, and later, he took me for a nice dinner. We sipped Cazadores tequila when we returned to my place. Hard liquor is like sodium pentothal to this man. Unusually deep thoughts and questions about women and sex sprung forth, and he revealed more about himself than he probably would have liked. The lovemaking that evening was warm and delectable; he had clearly listened to my comments. He is an enigma. Why he has felt the need to keep himself so guarded and cool for so many years is beyond me, when it is clear that he has affection for me. But I no longer feel the need to understand his behavior; we are both using each other to meet our own needs.

Moroccan Boy called while we were out at dinner. I can't imagine why he is still interested after all of this time; we'd make the oddest match. When it rains, it pours, and right now it's raining men (hallelujah!).

I am not in the mood for Monday morning paperwork and I am lingering at the café. The sun is out today after a horrible, snowy weekend. Gaby's newly arrived Cuban husband must be in utter shock, especially since the switch to standard time, with evening darkness arriving even earlier. It is nearly impossible to feel connected to nature in this ludicrous climate.

November 1st

I spoke to Paulo yesterday, and his mother does have kidney disease. He has been at the hospital in Havana with her for the past four days, and they will move her back to Cienfuegos for treatments. He is close to her and is extremely concerned and stressed with the arrangements, so this was the focus of our conversation.

November 3rd

Thank God it's Friday. It's *après* work and I am at home, resting in quietude, reading and writing. I have been reflective this week and have preferred to stay home alone.

Alejandro has been writing from different cities on the band tour and is anxiously awaiting our rendezvous. Oddly, I have had two potent dreams about him, unusual dreams for me. I wonder if I will still be attracted to him after two years. He obviously remembers the night clearly. His daily emails are affectionate.

Paulo's letters have still been arriving regularly. He is under pressure with his mother's diagnosis and the time spent at the hospital. He was rather terse about my questions in regard to the cost of apartments in Havana, but sent a short letter yesterday filled with Latin love talk. Naturally, we are having trouble comprehending each other's lives. Possibly, he is influenced by his friends, with tales of how incredibly rich all foreigners are ... or who knows what else? For this reason, he may not understand my financial constraints. Such is life, and such are the challenges of a long distance, foreign love affair.

November 6th

A Chinook wind blew in yesterday. The sun was blazing, and it was spring warm out—what an astounding difference in my mood and energy. The winters have a strong effect on my biorhythms.

Miguel called twice while I was out last night. I called back, and in conversation, told him I was going away for Christmas as well.

"Where? Mexico or Cuba? Are you going just to get lucky?"

I deflected, "Well, why are you going to Chile?"

"It's my homeland. But I think your trips are for trouble."

He speaks as though he wants me for his own, but will surely never say so.

Alejandro sent me the band's confidential itinerary. He has arranged to have two tickets at the door for the Calgary show. I wonder what he will say when he finds out I was in Havana in September.

Anna will be coming to Havana while I am there and has agreed to bring the laptop to Cuba for Paulo. If I bring both laptops, one may be confiscated. Recently I have had mixed feelings about the trip. Old memories are creeping up. When I left for France, my suitcase was filled with Christmas gifts and decorations, so that Jean-François and his son and I could make a beautiful Christmas in France. I left all of those well thought out gifts behind and felt the fool for having been so enthusiastic, and then suddenly betrayed.

The scientific explanation about our emotions in the movie *What the Bleep Do We Know!?* clarified something for me. Our brains build pathways that are developed from the different chemicals (peptides, I believe) we release with each emotion. Some trails are deeply ingrained in our brains and tell us what certain situations mean to us. For example, feelings of lust may mean "pleasure" or "embarrassment"; feelings of success may signify "freedom" or mean "material wealth"; feelings of love could mean "joy" or "pain." These messages loudly alert our consciousness. I think I have love = betrayal roadways that are deeply etched and have not been reconstructed for years.

November 11th
Remembrance Day

Miguel called last night and obviously had his heart set on coming up today, but my mum is here for a visit. It's just as well. I have spent the past few days in a lusty haze from Alejandro's visit. He arrived early and asked if we could spend the day together before set-up. The chemistry was instantaneous, sparks igniting the minute he came near me. I really did not expect this at all. I thought I would have lost the attraction after two years, especially in light of the other two lovers. (These droughts really take their toll. Extensive irrigation is required.)

Alejandro remembered every detail of my apartment, the smell of it, and even the taste of the tea I served him the night we spent together, asking if I would brew some. I don't want to sound trite (or delusional); his English is halting and he explained the impact I'd left on him and how, for some reason, I'd remained fresh in his mind for the past two years. My worn business card was neatly tucked in his wallet, and his face was earnest.

He is an interesting and interested man. He told me more about Cuban life and about his life in particular, working with one of the most successful musical groups in Cuba. His was a drastically different perspective than Paulo's as a struggling, starving journalist. Alejandro said that by Cuban standards, he is a millionaire. He earns in one month what the average Cuban earns in three years. His group tours all over the world, so he gets to experience all the riches of life in other countries. He also has a small business sideline that is quite lucrative.

He asked why I had not emailed him prior to my trip to Cuba and said I had most likely walked past his home if I was staying in Old Havana. He told me the location, and as it turned out, I had walked past it many times. We conferred on the dates, but he was actually in Asia on tour at the time I was in Havana, so we would not have crossed paths anyway. Apparently, as a gimmick, the Hotel Nacional frequently posts false bulletins. In reality, the hotel has no intention of paying the band's standard fee for a performance.

While I prepared tea and treats, he wanted to see my books and read my poetry.

"I am confused. You are so happy and laughing all of the time, but these poems are so sad. I don't understand?"

I explained that they'd been written after a life-altering heartbreak.

With great reluctance, I returned him to the hotel for his journey onward. He has continued to send emails on the rest of his tour. I may not hear from him for months in view of the Internet problems in Cuba, or maybe I will never hear from him again, *mais, c'est la vie.*

November 16th

I am dispirited about the trip. Paulo's letters have had a desperate tone to them in the past few weeks, with too many explanations of how he and his family are in dire circumstances, and how he is financially responsible. Comments about the upcoming trip tell me he has expectations of a whirlwind holiday extravaganza. He was argumentative about the transfers to and from Havana. This week, his letter after our phone call crossed the line, and his wheedling was transparent. He wrote a ridiculous opening, saying that he wasn't asking for anything, but could I bring him a used laptop and cell phone? *Wasn't asking for anything?* I'd intended to surprise him with the laptop and now that is ruined. I did not appreciate the tone, the repetition, and the capitalization throughout, as though I wouldn't understand. He has begun a campaign for stuff and I see how the stories of his circumstances may have been written to tug at my heartstrings. He also wrote, for the first time, that he desires "to leave this shit country" and there's only one way for him to do it at this point—marriage. Why can't he leave well enough alone and graciously accept whatever I offer of my own volition?

His fervent insistence about the places we are to stay in leads me to wonder if he is getting a commission. I realize that when people are desperate and see hope in someone else, their focus is on the hope. But I am not his lottery ticket and I do not like the feeling of being played. I have written him a response and said I no longer think it is a good idea for me to stay with him. It would be too difficult to extricate myself if we were in the apartment together. He wants to embroil me in his complicated life and make me part of the solution to his problems.

November 17th

Paulo has not responded yet. He will most likely be upset if his well-laid plans appear to be in jeopardy. How he reacts will be the dealmaker or dealbreaker. I'd hoped for a carefree holiday fling.

Surprisingly, Alejandro emailed yesterday upon his return to Cuba. His roommate had also had a Calgary rendezvous, and both of them are scheming up ways to come back. I don't think it's at all possible, but it is a sweet thought.

Miguel has called twice this week and booked me for this weekend, and I am looking forward to it.

Does this sound terrible, having three love interests? I guess for you, who are used to the amorous activities of the French, the answer would be *non*.

The Cuban Chronicles

November 20th

Last night, I had Anna and Kyle over for my Mexican feast. I had spent a lot of time during the day happily chopping and preparing handmade tortillas, salsas and whatnot, while Miguelito studied. Paco, the Mexican chef who taught me the art of the tortilla, said that when you can get your tortillas to puff up, you're ready to marry. I've got the puff mastered, but no husbands on the horizon for as far as the eye can see.

I tried to be mindful of my feelings as I was cooking, consciously preparing the dinner with affection for my three friends, as in the movie *Like Water for Chocolate*. If water can be imprinted with feelings and emotion, as Dr. Masaru Emoto claims, then why not food? Last week, while making myself dinner, I was in an agitated mood, having just received Paulo's request email. It was the worst meal I have cooked in years, and the smell it left in the apartment was also terrible. The Mexican dinner, if I do say so, was delicious. Everyone ate too much—a good sign for a happy cook.

Miguel tossed, turned, and snored both nights. I don't know how women sleep with men full-time. They all seem to make so much bloody noise in the night.

November 21st

There has been no word from Paulo, but his daughter has written. I don't know her, so this appears to be part of the campaign. She wrote an affectionate letter filled with enthusiasm about meeting me in December. I had bad dreams all night long and did not make my normal Tuesday morning call to Cuba. I do not want to spend time debating on the phone. If I do not call, he will need to find a way to access the Internet and he can respond with an email before we speak on the phone.

November 23rd

My mum called last night to see if I'd talked to Paulo, and we got into an argument over him. I can't figure out why she is so much in favor of this relationship.

I am envisioning him languishing in a Cuban jail, having been taken away as a dissident. It sounds melodramatic, but in his last letter he wrote about a group of people who'd been dismissed from their jobs, and some had been taken to jail for illegal Internet activities. If I translated properly, one of the men dismissed was his friend, the computer scientist, whom he has been paying to use the office Internet. He seems to write a little too freely about his "shit country," his hatred of the government, and the situation there. I know the Cuban government closely monitors email, especially in businesses. How did they catch these Internet activities, if not through monitoring? His emails last weekend were filled with anti-patriotic sentiments. He speaks to his daughter daily, so he knows that she has emailed me.

Alejandro has emailed once more. I did not think I would hear from him again, but he wants to make arrangements to see me on my upcoming trip. The idea really appeals to me at this point.

I met with Carrie for coffee yesterday to give her the things I'd bought for baby Lola on my trip. She too is going to Cuba for

Christmas and invited me to go out with her group in Havana. It could be interesting; she is taking Lola to Cuba. The father has not acknowledged the baby, called, or written, and is married with a new child. Time will tell how this trip unfolds for everyone. Isn't it serendipitous that the one year I go to Cuba for Christmas instead of Mexico, so many women I know will be there at the same time?

Miguel called last night while I was in bed watching *The Secret*, but I did not pick up. Long phone conversations agitate me and his have been long-winded as of late. I try to make the hour before sleep a quiet time, either by meditating, reading, or listening to something positive and uplifting.

My ex called early this morning to pre-book me for a trip he is making here next week, weather permitting.

I've just opened my email, and Paulo has written a huge letter, but I need help translating it.

November 25th

I awoke to the phone ringing this morning and did not recognize the area code. I'd seen it on the display a couple of days ago, but thought it was some crazy telemarketer. I was in a deep sleep and picked it up—it was Gabriel, the Spaniard.

Without the help of body language and eye contact, it was a difficult conversation, some of which I did not understand. He said I still sound like an Andalucían, laughing and happy. I told him I am returning to Cuba for Christmas and he immediately asked if it was for a *cubano*. I sidestepped the question and he said, "You can't bring a Cuban into the hotel if you're staying there again." Not a stupid man, this one. He invited me to come for a Spanish holiday.

The transformation in my love life has my head swimming; within twenty-four hours, Alejandro emailed, Miguel called looking for me, Terry called to book a dinner, Kavel has written, Paulo emailed, and Gabriel called with the invitation. These visualizations and meditations do work. What you focus on does expand.

Back to the Paulo saga.... I am mollified after translating his rational response, but remain cautious. He'd made a quick trip to Cienfuegos because his mother had been admitted to the hospital again. Both his mother and daughter wrote letters to which I replied that I would not be meeting them. He painted a pretty picture of the apartment he has booked. I will leave things as they are and see how they progress—the trip is only three weeks away.

November 26th

I attended a private dress rehearsal of a Cuban dance production with a couple I met in San Miguel de Allende at the art workshop. Cassandra does figurative work and we were allowed entrance for photos. Her husband is involved with war protection armament for the Pentagon. My mind does not comprehend war and I have no frame of reference, so I asked as many questions as I could get away with over dinner. I asked how he feels being involved in war. He is passionate about it and thinks he has been and will be saving many soldiers' lives. It takes a different kind of person to travel the world negotiating with police, government, and secret services. Cassandra says his way of unwinding and numbing himself from the pressure is through a heavy television addiction. I suspect other issues underlie their marriage as well. This is her trade-off for the high income and lavish home, but I can see her seething under the façade; she will not be able to sell her soul for the lifestyle forever. I would rather be living in my humble digs. We all have such different realities.

There was a message from Malik when I returned. He is the amusing, younger Lebanese I dated when I first moved to this city. He used to dress in Hugo Boss suits, pick me up in his Mercedes, and take me for extravagant dinners. He would tell me about his plans to buy a restaurant. At the time, I thought he was blowing hot air; however, he has just purchased his second restaurant. I wonder what incited a phone call after all this time. When you put out the call of the wild, the herd hears, from far and wide.

November 28th

I am jotting down just a few lines while my car warms. I'm at le café and it is kick-ass, record-breaking cold right now. Even on US talk shows, they are talking about Calgary's temperatures. I don't want to make sales calls today, but I must. At this time of year, clients give me the "what in the hell do you want?" look. They are all extremely busy building products for Christmas.

Everyone's getting excited for the trip to Cuba. The throng of women I know going to Cuba for Christmas are Anna, her sister and two friends from Montreal, Darshana, Carrie and Gaby, and also Maria and Ashley, who will be visiting their Cuban husbands. I spoke with Paulo today and the weather in Havana is perfect right now. There will be an International Film Festival on while I'm there, and he's got a list of things to do in the city.

I am going to Edmonton if the roads improve and have been invited to stay on for the weekend after the workweek at Miguel's. He was scheming to arrange another rendezvous after that, before we leave for our respective Christmas vacations.

This is comical. When we were supposed to be an item, we never made plans like these.

November 30th

I had great fun buying toys for the kids in Cuba; the children have nothing to do with Paulo's requests and I still look forward to the pleasure of playing Santa. I am especially excited about bringing a sack of gifts to the little cigar boy. I am taking hot sauces, sweet chipotle sauce, and balsamic vinegar, since Cuban food is so bland. I spoke to Darshana this morning and discovered she'll be taking the same flight home as I will. She flies in Christmas day on the same flight as Gaby and Carrie. She's staying in Varadero at an all-inclusive, but will come to Havana. I'm going to insist she stay with me. On all her trips to Varadero, she's never been to the salsa capital, and I'm sure she will love it.

December 2nd
Frozen-Ass Cold

I am at a restaurant to meet my brother and family; they're probably stuck in a snow bank somewhere.

So far, the weekend at Miguelito's is like a mini-vacation. When we make love in his home, it's better. There is something different and more intense; he changes and softens in his own environment. We've enjoyed wonderful meals and last night I indulged in a bottle of Amarone for our evening. His new theatre-size television was awesome for watching a Mexican concert of a wildly popular balladeer. We both got a little tipsy on the delectable, so-heavy-you-could-bite-it vino, and the night ended with naked dancing in the living room, followed by a raucous romp.

This weekend I've had, by far, the most fun with Miguel since I met him almost five years ago.

December 4th

I'm glad to be alive today, and I mean that literally. I drove home last night, determined to be back for Patricia's graduation party from a personal growth seminar. Not turning back on the highway was one of the dumbest things I've done in a long time. The roads were horrendous, with trucks and cars littering the ditches, and once I realized the situation wasn't going to improve, I was in too deep to turn back. If I had thought it over for one minute, I would have called the road report before leaving, made my apologies, and stayed snuggled on the couch with Miguel instead of taking a six-hour drive on the highway to hell.

He called to ensure my safe arrival, and said he'd thought to suggest I stay due to the weather. The only reason he hadn't was because of his ego; he thought I'd misconstrue the suggestion.

He'd asked me on the weekend, "Are you getting too attached to me?"

My energies are scattered between Paulo, Alejandro, Gabriel, Kavel, Malik—my sole focus is not on him. I think he needs to ask himself the question he put to me.

Paulo has emailed Anna twice now to enlist her help. I made the mistake of sending him a forward, and her address was included. He wrote that he was worried that something was wrong and asked that she tell me to email him. Good God. It's embarrassing, and she thinks he sounds desperate; I wholeheartedly agree and find his blandishments a turn-off. It's as though he's placed all his money on this one race and is frantic for a win. Some of my family members argue that I should be patient with the poor man and carry on with my plans.

My concern is his reaction when I reiterate that this is only going to be a vacation fling. One lover is trying to deny any feelings for me, keeping his heart cool as he can; the other is acting the part of a love-crazed desperado.

December 5th

There are harried people all around me in the café, caught up in the Christmas mania of the season. There is much affluence here right now, and people behave differently than ten years ago. They indulge in an almost frantic consumerism.

I had agreed to phone Paulo this morning and the call was annoying; the lines were poor, and I had to repeat everything. The tone of the conversation was sickly sweet, and it irritated me. I felt claustrophobic.

After the call, I opened a simple but beautiful email from Alejandro. It made all of Paulo's long, convoluted letters seem all the more absurd.

December 7th

I awoke from a horrific nightmare in the middle of the night. I had a stomachache and couldn't return to sleep, as repetitive thoughts circled around in my mind.

I bought roses for my key accounts and had fun delivering the pretty packages. Everyone is happy to receive flowers, and one of my male customers didn't know what to think, saying he hadn't received flowers from a woman in years. Our company didn't even send Christmas cards this year to acknowledge their clients' business. How do they manage to prosper when they are so incredibly greedy?

Have you seen the movie *The Kinsey Report?* I caught it on TV and watched with fascination. The sexual beliefs of the average North American were from the Dark Ages as recently as the '50s. Kinsey single-handedly brought the reality of what happens in people's bedrooms out in the open to show the world that there is no "normal" and to shed light on sexual behavior that had been kept in the shadows of ignorance forever.

I somehow feel grateful to him for my own sexual liberation.

December 8th

This Cuban man does not understand me, although I have spelled out my intentions and feelings with blunt clarity. The closer I come to the trip, the less time I want to spend with Paulo. I reminded him that I want to spend time with friends and to also have time alone to write on the trip. He sent a five-part email waxing poetic, trying to convince me that we need to "focus on our relationship" and that *his* agenda is that I spend all my time with him, because I see my friends all year in Canada. First, there was the trip he wanted to take to Cienfuegos to introduce me to his parents and daughter. Then there was the computer and cell phone incident. Now he wants to "take" me to Trinidad, maybe for a couple of days, maybe rent a car ("very cheap, you know, only $40 CUC a day, I'm always thinking of your budget"), maybe go to Forest of the Pines for a day. He thinks that his scheme of our touring Cuba on my pesos would enchant me? How dense is this man? I wrote back to say I am confused; have you saved money to take these side trips? Of course he has not. He speaks as though we are entrenched in a relationship. I am fed up with him and I haven't even seen him yet.

I met with Darshana this morning and we've made plans to meet in Havana. She will stay with me for a couple of nights, no matter where I end up. She understood my feelings about Paulo's letters of late; she has a friend in Mozambique and the girl writes, politely demanding care packages. We want our generosity to come from our own hearts and enjoy the element of surprise. We do not want to give because a gift is expected, outlined and stipulated.

December 11th

How do you deal with your insomnia? I have been waking in the wee hours, my mind in turmoil.

I live to travel and always await my trips like a little girl at Christmas counting down the sleeps. But now I am uneasy and unexcited, stressed out by thoughts about Paulo. I've had a few ludicrous disagreements now with family about the arguing and miscommunications with him.

Soon enough I will be in Cuba, and we will see how things unfold.

Six
Durmiendo con el Enemigo

© Wanda St.Hilaire

It is better to die on your feet than live on your knees.
—Emiliano Zapata
Mexican Revolutionary

December 19th
Varadero, Cuba

Amiga,

Grab a drink and sit down....

I arrive at the airport. The lines move slowly through customs as they grill everyone, making me remove my glasses and lift my hair from my face. I see Paulo waving madly and smiling through the sliding doors as I line up to exchange money. I am greeted with bear hugs and effusive kisses. He looks me over approvingly and says I look younger (I am in low cut jeans) and have lost weight.

"More pretty than before."

My Spanish has improved, and he is amused. He grabs my hand and leads me to meet a young Ukrainian couple from Canada whom he has met and has hooked up to stay at Ricardo's *casa particular*; they have come on a last minute flight with no reservations. We share a taxi.

After settling in, we go out to dinner with the couple. She is a flawless beauty of maybe twenty years old. He is lean and well-built. His tiny, close-set eyes make him look a little rodent-like, in striking contrast to her exquisiteness.

We decide on the nearby thatched-roof restaurant, and Paulo suggests I order his food. He unnecessarily shares his steak with each of us and finishes the balance of his meal in nanoseconds, while the rest of us enjoy a leisurely pace of dining over conversation. Am I imagining it, or does he have a look of martyrdom on his face as he sits with his empty plate while we have only begun our meals? It irritates me that he has inhaled his meal, quite probably trying to intimate that he should order seconds. If he is eating once a day, as he wrote, it is calorific food, because he has maintained a hefty weight. The couple leave shortly after dinner, and we stay and talk for a while.

We stroll back to the *casa* and when we return, I give him the large red stocking I have stuffed full with small gifts. Somewhere in the back of my mind, I do this to appease him. He appears pleased with the presents and is fascinated with the stocking. He seems not to have ever seen one before. I pull out the dog treats I have brought, and he suggests we go test them on the street, certain that Cuban dogs will not like them. There is no dog food in Cuba, only scraps and leftovers of rice and beans and the odd bone. Within minutes, two dogs saunter by, and, just as he predicted, they spit the food out, looking up at me in complete confusion. They march off in disgust. In spite of my objections, Paulo takes a bite out of one of the dog sausages and tells me they do not recognize this deluxe food with actual meat in it, and I realize how naïve tourists can be.

I grab my purse and ridiculously take a small suitcase filled with gifts to the bathroom to keep there while I take a shower. I am not really sure why I have done this, and he makes a huge to-do about it. What kind of a thing is this to do? This shows no trust. What do I think he will do—steal my things? I tell him that sometimes people are curious about their Christmas gifts and open them under the tree to sneak a peek.

"*No.* I have honor and respect your privacy! I weel not open your bags."

I realize I have had it in my mind for a couple of weeks to keep close guard on my purse when with him.

We do not have sex, firstly, because there is a warning signal in my belly that yells no, and secondly, because I hear a nagging voice of loyalty in the recesses of my mind. I uncharacteristically swaddle myself in clothing for bed. He kisses me passionately before we fall asleep and reluctantly accepts my excuses. I am turned on by his size and strength, but at the same time afraid of how easily he could overpower me. How does my body have the ability to respond physically to his kisses, yet still feel ambiguous about him? This must be the appeal of the archetypal Bad Boy in romance novels—a woman is ravaged in the days of old by a handsome yet evil pirate. She has fear and loathing in her heart, yet a stirring in her loins.

I have forgotten that his snoring could break the sound barrier and I prod him to change positions all night long. If only for this reason, I cannot sleep in the same bed with this man. He can sleep on the spare mattress tonight and then—in Havana—no more. I am exhausted when he awakens and, thankfully, he leaves the room so I can sleep.

He brings in a typical Cuban sandwich, and tells me he has made it especially for me. I am not sure what they make the yellow-tinged bread from here.

"Eat, eat. Do you want a coffee?"

"No, thank you."

"But I make you a coffee," he says with another simper.

"Okay, *café con leche, por favor.*"

Fifteen minutes later, with a flourish, he presents a small package of Cubita coffee. "I went to the store and I bought it for you!"

I thank him, but I am irritated by what appears to be a performance. I am still tired and wish I could sleep longer—I've never done well when organically challenged by lack of food, quiet time, or sleep.

Later, he brings in a small espresso without the milk I requested, and it is laden with sugar. My mouth puckers automatically; I never drink coffee with sugar. He is annoyed.

"I will drink it. It's fine."

"I can get milk."

"No, thank you. This is fine."

I can see he expects me to tap dance in fits of gratitude and does not think I have shown enough. I sense that he is not finding pleasure in doing this for me; he is doing it only to prove something. His pained expression contradicts his actions.

He comes back to see if I want a soft drink. I tell him for the umpteenth time that I do not like sweet drinks.

When I finally rise and shower, I notice a bruise on my shoulder. I look closer in the mirror, but it is not a bruise; it is a hicky. Upon further inspection, I discover I have a ring of bruise-like hickies around the front of my neck and shoulder. It looks as though someone has attempted to strangle me and it is vaguely disturbing. I did not realize his kisses were that strong.

In the kitchen, Ricardo is in his usual daytime drinking stance. In a childish, show-off manner, Paulo takes charge of the stereo and blasts the salsa music. After this many years in sales, I am hypersensitive to body language (sometimes to my annoyance) and I can see that Ricardo is displeased. I suggest to Paulo that he leave the remote in Ricardo's charge.

"No, es normal en Cuba. Ricardo es my friend and I can touch the music."

It is obvious that Ricardo does not agree. As with so many other things, he says, "Es normal en Cuba," but I wonder if it is normal only for Paulo. We are going to the beach and I watch as he pours a rum and Coke to take with him. Has he been drinking already this morning, I wonder. Ricardo tells him to be sure to bring the glass back, and I ask him what he will do with it at the beach. It's fine, he says, no problem.

He is clearly not enjoying our walk along the beach. He is restless, and his erratic, pinball machine energy is that of a man filled with frustration. His face once again has an anxious, pained look on it, and the definition of "antsy" fits: tensely nervous or apprehensive and moving or squirming around in a restless, bored, or impatient way. He becomes argumentative. The conversation is surreal and ridiculous. He blathers on and every sentence is grounds for a dispute in his mind. He raises his voice, and just as I had felt the capitalization in his letters was loud and aggressive, I find the same in his manner of speech right now. Also, he is repeating himself to the point of absurdity. What is wrong with him? I am confused, and this behavior is stirring memories that are constricting the pit of my stomach.

He asks if I will put the glass in my purse, but I am carrying a tiny bag and I say no. He throws the glass—Ricardo's glass—under a large palm tree. I ask why he has done this, and he says he is testing me: he wanted to see if I would carry it for him and I failed when I said no. I process the idea of his "testing" me. My shoulders tense in reflex.

The day is beautiful, and the ocean is an intoxicating turquoise, but the beauty is shattered with his tirade about how hard he had to work by the sweat of his brow, setting aside half of his money for "de life" and half for my trip, so that he would be able to make me a big dinner for my birthday (he has already mentioned my birthday dinner three times). He speaks about what sacrifices he has had to make to come here to meet me.

It incenses me that he is carrying on in this martyred tone and I tell him this trip is something I have to work for much, much longer, to cover financially. He prattles on, pushing me past tolerance. This is insanity. How did I get to this beautiful beach, just to squabble with this ridiculous man? I arrived last night, and this is the scenario at noon today.

"Look, this isn't going to work. Once we get to Havana, let's part ways," I say.

He is stone silent. We walk for a long time along the water's edge. He wants to use the bathroom at a beachside café. Will I wait? I sit bewildered, watching the diamond-like shards of sunlight flicker over the water. He comes back with a beer for himself and a sweet mango juice for me. I want neither to drink it nor offend him and he makes another fuss, saying that I don't like it.

He lamely attempts to redeem the situation and tells me he loves my earrings. They are new, he says; I didn't have them last time. I don't argue with him. He then invites me for a spaghetti lunch.

"You want to take me for lunch?" I ask to be sure I've heard him correctly.

"What! You don't believe that I invite you? I work hard to have de money for when you come. I have dignity!"

Yada, yada, yada.

On the street, he offers to brush the layer of sand off of my feet and notices for the first time the large red spot on my foot.

"It was not there last time."

"Yes, it was there. You just didn't notice it," I gently say.

"*No.* It was not there."

He has been peppering the conversation with platitudes, telling me he is going to show me how much he loves me and what he is going to do for me in Havana: make me breakfast in bed, make me nice dinners, take me out to special places, wash my clothes. *Wash my clothes?* Give me a break. He is behaving like a sycophant. These declarations make me even more uncomfortable and are highly incongruent with all the quarrelling. I am reminded of a wise piece of advice I heard in a lecture by a male professor: When romantically involved with a man, never pay attention to what he says. Pay attention only to what he does.

We stop at the new Casa de la Música nightclub and he asks to see the manager for a tour of the club. I catch only a few phrases of the rapid conversation, but his pitch and posture indicate an attempt to appear like a hotshot. When we leave, I ask him what the conversation was about. I am curious. He says his aunt is the manager of this chain and tells me her career history. He says we should come back tonight. I hedge.

"I invite you."

I say nothing, but wonder where in the hell he will get the $50 cover charge, which is double his monthly wage. The only way he can do this, I assume, is if he has fast-talked his way out of the cover. He repeats the story of his aunt not once, not twice, but three times. His behavior is obnoxious. My head swims, and I am at a loss as to how to handle this situation.

We go back to the same little restaurant for lunch. He orders and boasts to the owner that he is going to pay. I am embarrassed and at the same time sympathetic to the condition of the Cuban male under this God-forsaken regime. He has another beer with lunch.

He asks me three times, "How es your spaghetti?" How irritating can one person be?

When I get up to use the bathroom for the second time, he asks if I know where it is. I have used the bathroom here the night before as well as on the last trip. Why is he asking me this? I am quiet at lunch because I want no more bickering and although I am unsure of how to deal with him, I know I must tread lightly. How do I break away from him? He is acting like a person with a mental illness. Is he bi-polar?

The bill-paying is done with fanfare, and when the waiter brings the change, Paulo makes an even bigger production of being insulted.

"I am a gentleman!" he says, as he adds a single peso to the change.

He carries on, but I can't comprehend his nattering. It is fucking inane. All I know is that he is going to great lengths to show off to me and to the staff, and I want to stick my face in the sand. After he pays, he takes two ice cream bars from the freezer. I say no thank you (I told him twice last night that I did not like ice cream bars, but he bought one anyway). He makes a face at the waiter that conveys "what an ingrate" and then insists that I have something else. I take a bottle of water to shut him up. He hails a taxi—an unnecessary expense, since we can easily walk back to the *casa*.

We arrive, and Ricardo, mildly drunk, is impatiently awaiting our arrival at the door. He says Paulo had promised to bring back a bottle of rum when we returned, because Paulo had drunk half the bottle before we left. My mind registers this information. He consumed half a bottle of rum for breakfast?

Paulo asks to borrow $5 CUC and tells me six times he will pay me back, do I understand, *do I understand?* I do not want to buy a bottle of rum for these two nincompoops, but I give him the money because Ricardo is not taking no for an answer. I ask Paulo if he is going to have another drink, and does he remember that we are supposed to go to the bus station to buy a ticket for Havana?

"Noooooh," he says with his typical strong inflection, which is now repulsing me. Of course, he is not going to have another drink, and yes, he remembers we are going to purchase our tickets for Havana. He leaves to buy the rum, and I go to the room to freshen up. When I return, they have moved to the patio, and beside Paulo sits a strong, fresh drink.

He uses the bathroom and leaves our room door and bathroom door ajar. I am not paying close attention, but Ricardo is infuriated and asks Paulo why he has left the doors open where his daughter or wife could see him? Paulo disputes this; he is sure he closed the bathroom door. They argue. He sits and shakes his head, with a stupidly sad puppy face, and I finally tell him to let it go. Just apologize and forget it. There's nothing more illogical or idiotic than an argument between two men drinking. It was over alcohol that I ended my short marriage to a man I loved dearly and I ask myself, what on God's green earth am I doing here between these two fools?

I tell him I want to go to the bus station.

"No. We will call," he flatly states with an "end of discussion" tone.

I need to leave this midday drinking binge and get out in the Varadero sun. I want to ensure I have a ticket for tomorrow for Havana, where we can part ways. I go to the gate, and Paulo shouts for me to wait. He slams back his rum and ambles to the walkway. He drags his feet as slowly as possible and is in a full-scale man pout.

I try to ignore him for as long as possible, but cannot tolerate this childish behavior for one second longer. "What is your problem?"

He explodes.

"I do not like to walk why should I walk four kilometers when I can phone I want to stay at Ricardo's you are selfish all you think about es yourself always yourself yourself yourself you didn't like my coffee this morning and you make a face for the sugar I make you a sandwich for God's sake I took you for lunch and even paid for a taxi you think you are so special better than anyone else do you think you are perfect?"

I have entered the Twilight Zone.

People stop to look at us. I run across the street to get away from him, back toward the *casa*, and my head is spinning, spitting out little sparks of disbelief. This man barely knows me and this is how he is speaking to me? I need to get back to the *casa*. Now.

He runs up to me yelling, "Listen to me. Listen to me!"

His diatribe becomes thunderous—"Walking es stupid and you are stupid you don't understand anything I tell you I can phone but no you want to walk I tell you dat de dogs in Cuba won't like de dog food you brought but you don't listen I know Cuba I know de life and …"

I no longer hear anything now except the deafening rush of adrenaline in my brain. My eyes register the fact that every single person on this busy street, Cuban and foreigner alike, has stopped to look, mortified.

"*Listen to me!*"

He rushes at me as he screams with such force that he is frothing, his fury about to pop the throbbing veins on his forehead, but I keep walking fast. He grabs both of my arms in a way intended to hurt me.

"Don't touch me," I say slowly, firmly, and quietly. His eyes are insane. I now see I am in danger. "I will call the police."

Old fears that have lain dormant in cells seep through my body and bubble to the surface of my mind. I know what a man in this state is capable of. Get to the *casa*, I think, just get to the *casa*, be calm, and then quickly, but not too quickly, round up my things so that he does not destroy them, then ask Ricardo for help to keep me safe from this lunatic.

My feet do not move fast enough, and after what seems like an eternity, I arrive. Only after I close the door to the bathroom located inside our room do I realize I have made a fatal error in judgment; he has the key and can lock me in the room. *Please God, no.* When I come out of the bathroom, I see in his eyes that he has done just that. I check the door. It is locked. My stomach flips and my solar plexus constricts.

"Please unlock the door."

"No. Go sit down on de bed."

"Please. Unlock the door," my voice now quivers a little.

"NO. You sit down on de bed," he commands.

"Please unlock the door." I am on the verge of panic. "Please. Please. Unlock the door."

My fright infuriates him, and he suddenly grabs my arms like a vise and yells into my face. I now understand that he is a bitter man, and the chip on his shoulder from his circumstances, his life, is colossal. His plan has failed, and he is desperate.

"Oh, you think I am killer?" he says, mocking my fear.

I am now on the brink of hysteria. All of my childhood terrors are here, right now in this room, like scary monsters, and I whimper softly in realization, "Oh God. You are going to hurt me."

He does not hear me. My head is spinning. I plead with all my might, *"Please open the door."*

"Okay. You sit down on de bed and pay me for de lunch and I open de door and go to Havana," he says maliciously.

Oh my God, he is crazy. My suspicions that he is obsessed about money are true. I cannot go further into the room, because I know I will be trapped without recourse within these cement walls in the back of this house.

I have a powerful, body-wrenching flashback. My head bursts from this unexpected memory, and my entire body begins to tremble.

I tell him that I promise I will pay if he opens the door.

"*No!*" he yells once again menacingly into my face.

We go back and forth—I beg him to let me out, and he yells no. I desperately need help and bang on the stained glass to attract the attention of Ricardo and Malita.

Where are they?

How can they not have heard us?

At last, I see shadows outside the door. I say I will break the glass if he doesn't let me out, but he says to go ahead. He looks ready—I have seen this look before—so I let out a blood-curdling scream and smash at the door. My scream echoes in my head.

Finally, they open the door. I run to Ricardo, my body shaking uncontrollably, and I cry in huge sobs, gasping for air. Malita helps me move all my things into her daughter's room, and I can barely carry anything; I am trembling so badly. I drop and smash a bottle of hot sauce on the tile floor and forget some of my things and ask her if I can go back, because I know he will destroy anything I leave behind. She asks me what I would like them to do, *en español*, and I ask, please, that they send him back to Havana.

He and Ricardo are discussing things, to no avail. These two drunken men will never come to rational terms, because Paulo is an angry, desperate man, and Ricardo is a Cuban who thinks this is just a little domestic dispute that can have a kiss and make-up resolution. I am locked in the little room while this endless charade continues, my mind reeling in a state of shock.

Malita returns to the room and sees I am still shaking like a leaf and asks if I want a pill to calm my nerves. I remember that for some reason I have put an inordinate number of Ativan, normally reserved for turbulent flights, in my purse. I take one.

I have been contemplating giving him money to get rid of him, but why should I? He wants a refund for the one pathetic little lunch he has paid for?

I realize this train of thought is foolish; this man is a desperado and if he thinks he has lost one peso to implement his plan, he will be obsessed. Something has changed in his life since September, but I will never know what. I give Malita a handful of peso bills and ask her to give them to him. She is confused about why I am giving him money, but agrees.

I am trapped in the room like a caged cat. I cannot believe that I had a foreboding, but did not listen to my intuition. I knew in my gut that I should cancel our plans, but I listened to others and overrode my own inner voice. Friends asked why I was not excited about the trip and did not seem like myself. Now I realize it was because I was betraying my own reason. I did not trust this man as far as I could throw him after his letters changed, but I still chose to meet with him. I know full well that when someone needs to tell you how honorable he is, he is not. And I know that when a person says he will never lie to you, he is doing exactly that. I could easily have made reservations elsewhere, and he would not have known if I had arrived or not. Why had I not listened to myself?

I am having waves of déjà vu: it is my birthday, ten years ago exactly, and I am alone in a strange country, dazed and confused after a terrible, gut-wrenching experience with a lover turned traitor.

Am I stupid?

Ricardo comes to the door and asks please, will I speak to Paulo again; he thinks I should give him one more opportunity. I find out later he has been crying crocodile tears to enlist Ricardo's sympathy and support. I have absolutely no intention of giving him another chance, but decide it is best to say good-bye face to face, or he will never leave the house peacefully; he has too much to lose and will not give up easily. I agree, but insist that Ricardo stay in the room. Paulo tries to convince me into going back inside our room to talk "privative," and I flatly refuse. I am trembling again and I only want this over with. He is now completely drunk and is talking even further nonsense, and I ask him to leave.

"What do you want? What do you want? What do you want?" he keeps repeating.

"For you to *leave*."

He does not want to hear this and when Ricardo is turned the other way, he says quietly, with venom, "If you come to Havana, there will be beeg trouble for you. If you go to de hotel, I will find you. I have de connections."

"Did you hear what he just said, Ricardo?"

Ricardo is absorbed, looking at my assortment of sauces on the dresser. "No."

I repeat the threat and tell him of Paulo's demands for money when I was locked in the room. Paulo denies it.

"No, no, you must be mistaken. A real man would not say that," Ricardo says.

"No, I am not mistaken. Please leave, Paulo."

Three times, he tells me I must pay Ricardo for the room, and I say of course I will pay (not realizing that he wants me to pay now, so that he can coerce a commission from Ricardo later). He says he has paid a deposit on the apartment and he wants it back, but I know for sure he has paid nothing, because he would not risk it, and does not have it anyway. In a last-ditch attempt, he says the money I have given him is not enough to get to Havana (it is more than enough—it is well over a month's wage); he needs more. And how is he supposed to get to Havana at this hour? Take the train, I say, the same way you came. I want this conversation to end and I ask Ricardo to please make him leave. Ricardo finally maneuvers him to the door and before they exit, Paulo starts threatening, bellowing, and pointing his finger in a fury.

"*Don't you ever come back to Cuba! It weel be a problem for you!*"

Ricardo now sees that I have not exaggerated and he tells Paulo this is terrible behavior and forces him out of the room. Malita comes to help remove him and locks my door.

I hear Ricardo tell him to shower and leave. I hear his daughter in the hallway, home from school, and I see the doorknob rattle. I am in a scary movie. Is it the daughter?

"*¿Quién es?*" I say, but there is no answer. I hear someone walk away.

I hear noise, but do not know what's happening. I am a hostage locked in this room in Cuba. I hear Paulo take a shower.

Minutes later there is a light knock at the door.

"*¿Quién es?*" I ask three times but I am so fucking confused and the Ativan has taken effect and I think it is the little girl and I open it.

FUCK. OH. MY. GOD.

It is Paulo. He looks like Robert DeNiro in *Cape Fear*.

I try to close the door and he forcefully jerks it open, repeating, "*Es this relaxshunship over? Es this relaxshunship over?*"

"Yes!" I say while gripping the door with all of my might, horrified that he will succeed. Images fly through my mind of what he will do to me if he gets in.

"*Don't come back to Cuba!*" he yells, as he tries to tear the door open, and in a rush of self preservation, I smash his hand in the door, over and over and over, hard, and finally Ricardo has heard and pulls at him, and I shut the door, but it is like a very bad nightmare. I cannot move and I cannot make the door lock and my heart is pounding out of my chest and I am so terrified that I cannot believe this is real.

Later, when I return to my room, the one small thing I forgot—a box for my soap—I find crushed in a corner.

December 20th

Happy Birthday to me.

    Paulo finally left after threatening to fight with Ricardo and report him to the police for having tourists stay illegally in his home. Ricardo informed me that Paulo has a Cuban girlfriend, a poor woman, who has been calling him for help with Paulo and his bullshit. She has been in an off-and-on relationship with him for some time. I did not for one minute expect a Cuban lover to be monogamous (I wasn't), but the presence of the girlfriend makes his crusade of endless love even more deceitful. It explains why he came with his little briefcase almost empty on this trip, as compared to the last time when he came with a full travel bag. Paulo pounded at Ricardo for money, money, money—he was completely obsessed. He insisted earlier on a commission for the young couple's room, all the while professing his and Ricardo's deep friendship. This is most likely how he was able to buy me lunch and pay for the taxi. I am sure he had a hefty commission at stake with the apartment in Havana.

    There is more, but I cannot even write it; Ricardo himself was inebriated, so who knows what is fact and what is fiction, with his opinion skewed by alcohol. I suppose it is unimportant. What is important is that I am okay and that I did not end up with him in Havana, where I would have been extremely vulnerable hidden in the backstreets.

    God forbid.

A chatty, toothless, horse-cab driver gave me a long ride along the *avenida* for only a fraction of the normal rate today. I told him he was a kind man. "No, you are kind. And so pretty!" he responded. This random act of kindness from a stranger was much needed today.

The Ukrainian couple returned from the beach and thoughtfully accompanied me on a long walk to the store. They want me to stay on at the *casa*. I was relieved to speak with someone in English. They'd been suspicious of Paulo's friendliness at the airport and were happier than he when I made it through customs, because they saw me as a nice Canadian woman who would be going to the *casa particular*. He'd told them I was his Canadian girlfriend and that he planned on marrying me. So there we have it. Unfortunately for him, he chose a perfect candidate for a foreign fling, but an unlikely candidate to lure into a Cuban marriage.

The connection was poor when I called my sister to let her know what had transpired since my arrival, and that plans have taken a turn.

I am afraid he will return. I want to go to Havana, but I don't know where to stay. Malita has a friend with a *casa particular* in the neighborhood of Vedado, and it is not an area Paulo frequents, but there is not much of interest to me there. He knows where I like to go in Old Havana, so this is my dilemma. Am I safer at a secure hotel in Old Havana or in Vedado, out of his territory? Should I contact Alejandro, or would that be ridiculous?

Unfortunately, Myrna's predictions were chillingly accurate:

Does Paulo love Wanda as he professes: No.

Does he consider her a meal ticket: Yes.

Should Wanda return to Cuba: No. No. No.

Malita told me that Paulo has called five times today. He is still in Varadero and has slept in a park and says it is my birthday and he wants to see me. He thinks he can still convince me to go to Havana with him.

Fuck.

I am not out of the woods yet.

Malita is going shopping, so I will go to the beach instead of risking the possibility of being trapped here again and under siege.

I rent a chair near some guards, and two young Israeli men invite me to sit and chat. I feel safer sitting with them, since I am at a section of beach near the *casa* that is sparsely populated. One of the men speaks fluent English and is drop dead gorgeous; the other is sweet and homely.

They tell me of their experiences in Havana—these guys have been taken every which way you can imagine. It is partially self-inflicted, because the gorgeous one wants to get "hooked up" with beautiful girls, and partially because they are marks. They have a lot of money and no travel savvy, and the land sharks can smell it. They have been hustled by half of Havana and escaped, as they put it. I think they are idiots with their money, but then, I am an idiot with love. They tell me of a woman from England at their *casa particular* who was crying for days because her new Cuban boyfriend (whom she most likely slept with first) stole her purse with all her money, along with her passport and identification. They gave her money, and fortunately her traveler's cheque replacements arrived. This sickens me further. I once said to Vicki, prior to coming back here, that Cuba is a nation unto itself. Now I see how true it is. A friendly fellow sitting with a large group of young men walks by and tells me he is from Calgary.

"Ask them if they speak Arabic," the gorgeous one asks of me.

I ask, and yes, they are Lebanese. They join us to discuss cigar buying and whatnot in Havana. A crew of swarthy men surrounds me. The first friendly one, Jamal, starts a side conversation with me and we discover that he is the cousin of Malik, the guy I dated long ago who, ironically, as I mentioned, called me only two weeks ago. A few of the others are related to Malik as well and they can't believe it. I think they are surprised, since Malik dates only Lebanese women when he is around his family. Two say they are going to call him when they get to the room, to tell him they met me, and I give them one of my bookmarks so they don't forget my name. Malik will be surprised.

The conversation takes a sordid turn because Gorgeous, now in the company of men, feels free to talk of his escapades with women in Havana. This line of conversation does not appeal to the young Lebanese, who are almost all engaged and Muslim, except for the fascinated fat one who is single and wants to know how he can find women. The Israelis brag of all of the women they have fucked in their short visit. Jamal is squirming and ill at ease with the ribald conversation, especially when Gorgeous, who is, I now realize, an utter bastard, says something excessively crude and vulgar at the end of one of his stories. He laughs as he says that one of the girls turned out to be fourteen. These jerks deserve to be taken, I think. Jamal gets up to leave and looks at me sympathetically, then invites me to join them at a nightclub tonight and says he would be truly pleased if I came. His eyes are kind and he looks like a decent human being. I have been cemented to the chair in a stupor and I get up to leave in slow motion, depressed further by the ugliness of the stories I have just heard.

I return to the *casa*, and it appears that the asshole has gone to the police to report Ricardo. Talk about the pot calling the kettle black. There is an enormous fine if they get caught, and Ricardo is now worried sick, pacing like a cat and smoking like a fiend. Malita is going to go to wherever you go to make a bribe. Joy to us all.

Miguel called late the night before I left, to wish me well once again. Now, in this absurd situation, I long for his simplicity and his straight arrow personality, even though he can sometimes seem so ordinary. Not once have I ever sensed he was lying, even if the truth was not what I wanted to hear.

This Cuban crisis helps me understand better why most people take the road well traveled.

The Cuban Chronicles

My sister was to call the *casa* at 5 p.m. I picked up the phone at five sharp and imagine my surprise to hear a man's voice say, "Happy Birthday!"

It was none other than my ex-husband. In her concern for my wellbeing, Lana called him and asked if he would come get me if need be. He told me he would fly to Cuba immediately if I wanted him to, but I said that it was totally unnecessary. Remember when she called him after the France Fiasco, and he came to Puerto Vallarta to make sure I was okay? I could almost hear him shaking his head in disbelief to discover that once again, I was in a foreign love predicament.

Lana called next and explained that she thought he would be the best man for the task, available to come get me at a moment's notice (she still holds him somewhat responsible for the turns my life has taken since our divorce, but I certainly do not). It is a comfort to have a sister who, in spite of her drastically different lifestyle, will not judge mine and will support me wherever I am, no matter what poo I land in. She called the Canadian Consulate, and they said that they do not take this type of thing lightly, and that I can email, call, or drop in twenty-four hours a day if I need any help at all. Let's hope not.

I learned a new word today—*fula*: a bad or fucked-up situation or person. This is both. I am drained and feeling foolish. I don't need to return to Cuba for a long, long time.

Malita offered to prepare us a dinner of lobster, potatoes, salad, rice, beans, and bread for this evening if we wish. It sounded to me like a wonderful idea, and the young couple agreed. They'd already planned to spend the evening with me for my birthday. They moved to Canada from Ukraine only a few years ago and speak heavily accented English, so Ricardo doesn't understand them well. He retired to the patio with his ever-present drink in hand. The dinner, prepared by both Malita and Ricardo, was delicious, the lobster plentiful, the menu exactly as promised. The couple bought cake for dessert, and I had some herbal teas with me.

We discussed life in Ukraine, and the girl asked me about Cuba, as she knew nothing about the country. I explained the little I know of the political situation and history of Cuba. Malita listened to our conversation as she tidied and told me that Cubans are not to discuss Castro, the *Revolución*, or politics. She told me emails are closely monitored for treason or subversive content. I told her of Paulo's recklessness in his emails, and she said he was playing with fire by expressing his hatred for the system in such a careless manner. That leads me to believe his emails were the reason his friend was fired, and he probably knew that he himself would not suffer the consequences of writing so freely, since he had no connection to the job.

We had plans to go to the open-air disco across the way, but it poured. It doesn't matter—I am exhausted anyway. I still have no idea what to do. I find Varadero too quiet, and staying at the *casa* is boring. Should I go to Havana soon, or will that psycho be prowling the streets looking for me, because he has nothing better to do?

My neck looks worse. I am ever so glad I did not sleep with him on night one.

December 21st

I awoke in the worst of moods today. Two men, one on either side of my little room, were horking up hairballs, coughing, sputtering, and pissing. I decided to bury my head under my threadbare pillow and go back to sleep. Why rush to get up?

I spent the day walking along the beach and tried to sit peacefully, but I did not enjoy the beauty. I was angry most of the day, angry at myself for being influenced and for being convinced that I was too harsh and mean with the "poor Cuban," but angry at Paulo. I should have cut the communication when I became uncomfortable with his letters and calls.

If the truth be told, our early parting was inevitable. I've had a niggling feeling since our first day together in Havana that this was a case of The Princess and the Pea. The pea buried under the thrill and the façade of romance was my unyielding belief about the rites of mating. I cannot buy this whole Cuban courting ritual; it is just too distasteful that a woman should need to pay a man's way. How did such a proud culture digress to this? Castroism has done a fine job of castrating its comrades, rendering them impotent to provide and thrive. The world seems upside down: too many of our men are not comfortable to act as nature intended them to; too many of their men are reduced to feeding off of foreigners.

On my walk along the *avenida*, I saw the Lebanese clan drive by on motorcycles. Further down the road, I heard my name called. It was Jamal. He and another of the group had been pulled over by the police for some imaginary infraction. I asked about the cuts and scrapes on his face. He and one of the others had been in an accident the day before. As well, two other members of his group, whom I hadn't met, had gotten into a fight in the nightclub. As the eldest cousin, he is in charge of the group and is having a hard time keeping them under control. It reminded me of the movie *Sideways*—would they all go home to their fiancées looking as though they had been in a car crash?

The men on the beach who tried to engage me in conversation today were completely unsuccessful. I wanted nothing to do with anyone. I appreciate that Ricardo is letting me stay on longer, but I have never liked the restrictions of B&Bs. Also, with the police on high alert, he would prefer for us not to come and go too much, and I find it annoying. He also insists that we come in the back way. Tonight I was semi-petrified walking through a pitch-black field to get to the back gate. As I rustled through the tall weeds, a cat leapt out of the underbrush, and I screamed, imagining it to be a giant lizard or a snake.

Today it struck me that maybe Lana had given my address to the consulate and that they had alerted the police. I hope to God she hadn't done it; reporting my whereabouts would be a mistake that could ruin these people's lives.

I hate being underfoot in the midst of a family's life, but the Ukrainian couple has integrated and taken over the house without a qualm. I guess it is a cultural thing. They ate tomato sauce and mayonnaise on yellow bread tonight for dinner. I am still stunned by the girl's beauty—her shiny long hair, flawless cream-colored skin, and perfect little Barbie body. When we met, I asked her if she was a model.

"Why do you ask that?"

"Because you are so beautiful."

"But you are not ugly! I hope I can look like you when I am your age."

I actually hadn't asked in the belief that I was ugly.

Her boyfriend has the strange idea that Monday night did not count as one night's stay, and that he shouldn't have to pay for it. He tried to explain his logic and wanted to argue the point. Another odd couple arrived to crowd the tiny *casita* even further— a sophisticated looking black woman and an old Yugoslavian man who gave me a loud lecture on the break-up of the Yugoslav—an added bonus to the shit show.

I wandered around the Barlovento today to inquire about a room. It was surprisingly empty for high season. It occurred to me that it would not make a bit of difference where I stayed. Why pay quadruple the price to be miserable? I don't really want to be anywhere on this island. A big part of the allure of Havana was the male attention and right now, frankly, my dear, I don't give a damn.

My plan for a siesta after the beach was spoiled by a surprise busload of loud relatives crammed into the *casita*. One shrill woman did not shut up, not even to breathe, speaking Speedy Gonzales Spanish for well over an hour. I wanted to scream obscenities out the door at her.

The night air seemed to clear my head a little after I took the long walk to La Vicaria restaurant, which Ricardo had recommended on my last trip. The meal was par for the course and the service atrocious, but at least they had good flan, a tiny piece of comfort.

I finally opened a book that one of my good clients gave me for Christmas. It is a travel book written by a Pulitzer Prize-winning journalist. It begins in your fair city.

December 22nd

It is ten in the evening, and I feel trapped at the *casa*. The streets of Varadero, as I mentioned last time, are not welcoming late at night. I have a raging headache anyway, so it is best to rest.

I ate my "breakfast": spaghetti—the eggs were mysteriously cut off early today—at my little *palapa* restaurant. Two days ago, the waitress overcharged me and I'd left a huge tip, not realizing it until later. The first night, the woman at the water stand charged me double; it is a typical practice here, and I'm not fond of it.

The helpful agent to whom I'd promised a book was not in Varadero, but I reached her on her cell and delivered the gift to the hotel, care of her colleague.

I overheard Ricardo and the young couple on the patio discussing Paulo while I was writing inside. Even though it shouldn't, Ricardo's opinion makes me feel worse, and I don't particularly want the couple filled in on the details; the situation is humiliating enough. Paulo called again today, belligerently demanding to know where I was and when I would be coming to Havana. Ricardo told him that I would be leaving tomorrow, but that he thought I was returning to Canada. Paulo may or may not buy the story, and I am once again concerned about the trip to Havana. Even Ricardo and Malita now consider him dangerous, and in their culture, a lot more domestic squabbling and violence are tolerated. Paulo either thinks he can win me back or wants to hurt me.

I had a quiet meditation this morning and then, through Malita, booked the *casa particular* in Vedado for Sunday. There is a new Internet place, so I checked my emails today, and there were two from Alejandro asking about my whereabouts. I spent one and a half painstaking hours writing two emails and replying to Alejandro (the machines are incredibly slow) and then found that the letters did not transmit. Malita, I discovered, has email but no Internet (which I didn't think possible—oh, the power of Big Brother), so I tried again tonight. Dar doesn't arrive until Thursday; I am counting the days to see her. I want to book a good hotel in Old Havana for her stay and will suss the situation out when I get there. I will try to negotiate on a taxi to Havana, instead of carrying all my bags to and from bus stations.

As I suspected, Ricardo is not thrilled with the young couple's infiltration of the house. They also do not understand the ramifications and the family's need to be discreet right now, and he wants to tell them to leave tomorrow. They rented motorbikes and did not return them tonight, wanting to get every cent's worth of their investment until the morning. They plan to leave the bikes on the street. Ricardo says there is a high risk of theft and then, police involvement. He has asked for my help in explaining the situation to them, and I agreed to do it, because I know they cannot afford the exorbitant Christmas rates at the hotels. I have been compliant, but am not too keen on the cloak and dagger situation either; however, I've not had the energy or inclination to move to a hotel.

The sunburned twosome returned from Matanzas today with handfuls of coral, sea cucumber, shells, and two crabs to take back to Canada. I squelched my dismay and tried to explain that customs would not permit the entry of these dead creatures, but they didn't understand. The concept of not taking these items for environmental reasons would really be lost on them, so I didn't embark on that discussion.

My Spanish, limited as it may seem at times, has been a godsend on this trip. I would have had one heck of a time with the Paulo incident had I not known some Spanish, and it was a necessity at the bank today. There was a huge line-up in the first bank and there were problems with Visa advances. When she realized I spoke some Spanish, a worker sent me to another bank tucked away on a nearby side street. The second one also had a line-up, and if I'd spoken only English, I'd have been there half the day. A Cuban bank is a serious place; one is made to feel guilty for merely exchanging money. I was required to sign in five places and had my passport taken away for a lengthy check. I broke the tension by kibitzing with the teller, and thankfully, my fair hair has its benefits for the line-ups. I don't know how the system works, so I'll accept the advantage. One needs to get a lot of cash at a time, because credit cards are almost useless, and the hassle at the bank deters frequent exchanges.

This has been one hell of an odd vacation so far. It has taken most of the day to do my business at the bank, use the Internet, and arrange the stay in Havana—things that should have taken an hour.

When I returned, Malita and Ricardo were getting pedicures from a woman who does in-home services. They suggested I have one too, but I took a closer look at her tattered kit; it was filled with antiquated tools and old polishes, and nothing in the box indicated she was sterilizing anything. I wanted to support her small business, but I was not about to risk picking up some bizarre tropical foot fungus.

Ricardo's handsome younger brother was here again last night, this time *sans* wife and son. He is a talkative, sparkling man, and watched me with an eagle's eye on the patio before coming out.

"Tonight, I am single!"

He was told (by Malita) in no uncertain terms to go home to his wife.

I walked a different route this evening and found that Josone Park is close by. The attractive guide at the entrance lifted my hair to smell my perfume, and I got a tingly skin rush—not dead yet. There are four restaurants in the park, and I chose the Italian restaurant, even though I'd had spaghetti for breakfast. I was seated at a wonderful table with a huge open window facing onto the pond and a view of the park. A trio played, and the energetic lead singer gave a dance lesson to a young Scandinavian woman at the only other occupied table. He grabbed me for a dance lesson, but was disappointed when he saw that I could dance. The group left, and I was happy for the solitude, but shortly thereafter, a flashy, tanned couple of unknown origin came in, and a British couple followed behind them. The British woman would not stop staring at me. I was not in the mood to be scrutinized. The smiling waiter was friendly and, in a first for me in Cuba, he gave me a free—and, another first—tasty salad. He dragged the staff out of the kitchen to meet me, telling them I was like a *cubana*. I guess he was referring to my Spanish and my inquisitiveness? I don't know.

I am in bed playing a Zen meditation track on the computer, and it is soothing. Taking advantage of a rare moment of privacy, I wrote on the tiny patio in the balmy night air, until something large and unrecognizable flew at me. I also knew Ricardo would not sleep until he knew I'd locked the door, so I came inside.

The travel book is excellently written (hence, the Pulitzer Prize), but too dainty for my liking. Much of the acclaimed travel writing I've read so far is academic, sweet, and poetic, but lacks candor, the nitty-gritty about when shit happens. (I mean, can the whole trip be full of fragrant fields of lavender and warm, fresh baguettes?) I admire the writing and aspire to such greatness, but must admit I love irreverent books, like the trilogy an American expat wrote about his misadventures living in Vallarta for the past twenty-five years. His writing is not particularly literary, but his stories are laugh out loud hilarious.

December 23rd

I began the day with what I think was a deep fried omelet. I thought of you in Paris, remembering how soft and delicious the omelets were. The French are masters of the *oeuf*. At least the *café con leche* was potable, and the bread was minus the yellow tint.

I had the feeling someone was watching me, but there was nobody in the open-air restaurant. I ate and read, but again could feel eyes upon me. I scanned for the source and jumped when I saw from a shuttered window to the right of me two eyes peering out intently between the slats, unblinking and unembarrassed.

The bathroom was a horror (and I've peed in many nightmarish *baños* in Mexico over the years), and I wished I could return to the *casa* around the corner. But I knew Ricardo would be pissed off if I came in and out once again.

I don't know why, but I am fascinated with Che's image and I keep buying Che cards and paraphernalia. It could be that I am falling for his heroic freedom fighter persona as the White Knight who tried to save Cuba, but who really knows if, had he lived, he would have joined the dark side.

The rare shade-seeker of the beach, I found a cool spot under a *palapa* to people-watch, and in the sand next to me I found an old five centavo coin with Che's image on it. Is he my Cuban St. Michael, protecting me from harm?

A young, well dressed black man walked at the shoreline, looking virile and strong. Next, a café colored man of approximately the same age walked past. He had an affliction that had bent and twisted his body in such a way that he could only look upward as he limped along. I could not imagine having to look skyward at all times and felt pangs of pain for him. There was such a stark disparity in the realities of these two men, I thought. An older French couple walked onto the beach and had obviously just landed, thrilled by the aqua water and white sand. A young Cuban with rippling abs and a Greek god stature sat in the surf for a long time, completely content. In contrast, a blonde woman of my age frolicked in the water in a thong cut too high, her flubbery bum jiggling all the while. I could not help but think that cellulite (which has not bypassed my body) is Mother Nature's cruel joke, and no matter which way you look at it, white, dimply skin is just not attractive.

Naturally, I have been pondering Paulo's behavior and reviewing the red flags that I chose to overlook for the sake of sexual adventure. I doubt that Ricardo's assessment of the situation is accurate; he's not the brightest star in the universe. He does not know what has transpired over the past few months; only I do. Paulo is a *Sleeping with the Enemy* man. I believe that aside from personal gain, he wanted to consume me, possess me, overpower me.

Just to clarify, *mon amie*: this is nothing like the despondent, inconsolable shell of a human you saw in Paris after the tsunami that was Jean-François. My mind is tired of the drama. I am disappointed over a ruined holiday. I am mystified that I placed myself in harm's way and did not listen to my soul's warnings. However, I did not engage my heart in this love story. I did not fall hook, line, and sinker into the deep end of the ocean as I did with my Frenchman.

Well, I've seen it all now. I walked further down the beach toward the *casa* this afternoon and stopped at a friendly little beach bar that I'd discovered yesterday. I bought a drink and sat down in the sand under a *palapa*. Two groups of Cubans were on either side of me as I lay down in my own little world enjoying the music. After an hour, a young black man from one of the groups came over. He persistently tried convincing me to meet him tonight at the Mambo Club. His friends began dancing, and he invited me to dance in the sand; he was an excellent dancer and before long, they had me in a *casino rueda* circle. This is like salsa square dancing. It made me want to dance tonight, but I am not going to meet this young stud and get caught up in more melodrama.

A grandmother was with the group. I assumed she was the *abuela* of the girl she was with; she was speaking fluent Spanish and had light brown skin like the girl's. She was dancing too, having fun. She provoked one of the young black men into a wrestling match and chased him around the sand, trying to flip him. I was amazed as I watched; she was flagrantly flirtatious, acting like a young girl as she chased this virile, twenty-something man. She was at least seventy-five years old and was heavy-set with a deeply wrinkled face and sagging body, but still incredibly strong. They later introduced me to her, and said she too was from Canada, Québec to be exact. She spoke no English, only French and Spanish, so we conversed in Spanish.

She lives in Cuba six months of the year and has a house in Varadero and one in Santa Clara. She is married to a Cuban. Ah—these must be his grandchildren, I thought. I almost fell headfirst into the sand when I discovered her husband is a thirty-four year old Afro-Cuban! *Mon Dieu.* I tried to picture my own British grandmother (who looked a lot like this woman) married to a young Cuban. The woman had come to Varadero out of spite, without telling her husband, because he'd been out partying too much, leaving her alone in the *casa*. No kidding. She acted as a young wife, angry with her wayward husband and anxious to exact revenge. I can't wrap my head around the story, but it demonstrates that if you think young, you can reverse at least some of the effects of aging.

There was a *quinceañera* in progress at one of the *casas* on the main street, and I stopped to watch the young girls in their pretty dresses. The *quinceañera* is a rite of passage into womanhood in some Latin cultures that is celebrated on a girl's fifteenth birthday. It is a wonderfully festive occasion, something I wish was part of our culture as well.

I must have looked more relaxed; three different men accosted me on the way home.

Let's add insult to injury. Ricardo, soused again, droned on about his expertise with women. While pointing at me, he stated that men his age prefer women over fifty.

"Are you talking about me?" I said, looking around, sure I'd find someone behind me.

"Yes."

Gracias, asshole.

He tried to redeem himself by telling me that I am elegant (they use that word a lot here) and must have been beautiful when I was young. He'd been bragging to the Ukrainian about all of his conquests as a young man, saying he'd had up to six girlfriends at a time.

"I think it is better to have one beautiful and great woman than a bunch of bad, ugly ones," the Ukrainian said.

Ricardo didn't really understand and I silently laughed at this jab. He outlined a curvaceous body with his hands, and with a curled lip, said that his wife was once thin, but now is fat, then laughed as he said, "No, es okay."

I itched to say, "Oh really, *panzón*." That is the word for a fat-bellied man, which Frida Khalo frequently called Diego Rivera, her toad-esque husband.

I am glad to be leaving the *casa* tomorrow. The young Ukrainian must have sensed my agitation and said not to worry; he thought I was much younger than fifty. At this stage in my life, I find the topic of age to be a sensitive one.

We'd all moved to the patio after dinner, and Ricardo and the couple got into a heated disagreement about leaving one's homeland to live in a different country. Ricardo and Malita have tickets for Miami and have arranged some type of forbidden exit. Ricardo has not worked in over fifteen years, instead earning his money illegally through the *casa particular*. He has had the freedom to sit on his ass and drink while Malita does the cleaning and cooking and he will now be faced with the harsh reality of a fast-paced, American work life. He thinks he will have no problem adjusting to the change. The Ukrainian commented that he found the transition to the Canadian culture and climate difficult, that he was depressed and missed his homeland. Ricardo told him that if he didn't like Canada, he should go back to Ukraine.

"I am forty-three. You are a child! You are twenty-three, you know nothing!"

He will soon discover that this young man knows a lot, that the adjustment to the US, especially at his age, will be extremely difficult. I was uncomfortable, as I am with any confrontation, and excused myself to talk to Malita. She is a warm woman and seems to be happy in spite of the fact that she lives with a loud-mouthed schnook. Maybe she's planning her own private escape when she gets to the land of milk and honey, the United States of America. She did laundry for me today, and my clothing was beautifully washed and pressed when I arrived back at the *casa*. We checked the email, and my two letters had gone through. I asked for permission to use the phone to leave a message with Alejandro's father as he'd asked me to do, but the man didn't understand a word. Malita confirmed my Spanish was correct when I spoke to him and she tried to repeat what I'd said, but still he did not understand. I was asked to call his father because I discovered that Alejandro is … married. What else did I expect?

    I gave Malita's daughter all the gifts I'd brought for Paulo's niece, and presented Malita with the gift originally intended for Paulo's sister. I handed Ricardo one of the caps I'd bought for Paulo, even though I knew he would not appreciate the gift. Sure enough, he pretended to throw it over the fence.

    "Jus kiddin," he quipped.

    I thought he'd gone to bed to pass out, so I slipped out to write on the patio. No such luck—he followed me out with a fresh drink. He rehashed the Paulo incident and gave me his brilliant insights on the situation. I wanted to flee, but no, I am too polite for that. His favorite words are "eees boolshit," accompanied by a shooing wave of the hand, and "fuck" (although admittedly, "fuck" is my word of choice on this trip too). He wants to give me his life history for a book; he thinks it will be Oscar material. Good grief, Charlie Brown. As soon as Malita flitted by, I made a breakaway. She tried to tell him to leave me be and go to bed. As she walked away, he pointed at his crotch.

    "What? Go to bed? She have de *menstruación!*"

    What an arse.

Seven
The Sound of Music (Salsa Music, That Is)

© Wanda St.Hilaire

You will find that the woman who is really kind to dogs is always the one who has failed to inspire sympathy in men.
—Max Beerbohm
English Caricaturist and Author

Christmas Day
Havana, Cuba

I am back at the terrace of the Ambos Mundos. It's been only one and a half days and I have much to tell.

The Cubanacan representative to whom I spoke with last week, and who had seemed rude, turned out to be helpful after all, and got me a transfer to Havana with a pick-up at a nearby hotel. One of the men from the beach *rueda* dancing was on the veranda. He was an attractive green-eyed black man—the one who'd been chased by Grandma Moses. He asked if I'd gone dancing with his friend at the Mambo Club and said he was awaiting his English girlfriend.

At the last stop before leaving Varadero, we picked up a group from Paris. I placed my bag obtrusively, to avoid company, but a cute, young Frenchman, carrying what looked like a purse to me, chose to sit beside me, smiling and arranging my bag between his legs.

"*Bonjour! Ça va?*"

"Ummmm... *Ça va bien merci, et vous?*"

My French files were tucked away deeply in the recesses of my mind, jumbled up with Spanish. I put on my earphones and let myself get absorbed in the music.

He was a Curious George and asked what I was listening to, intent on engaging me in some semblance of a conversation. His infectious friendliness forced me to drop my abnormal reserve. He offered his email address, in case I should come to Paris, he said. We shared my earphones the rest of the way to listen to music together and he was happily surprised to hear I had French music that he recognized. A semi-pro soccer player, he was traveling with his family and a friend and asked me to join them at Casa de la Música to dance; he hoped I would teach him salsa and suggested a rendezvous someplace first. I gave him the address of Taberna de la Muralla in Old Havana for that evening. It was certainly a more interesting ride than I would have had if I had taken a private taxi, as I had planned.

I had absolutely no idea where my *casa particular* was in Vedado and was relieved when the bus driver dropped me off in front of the apartment. Although I had left one bag behind in Varadero, my backpack and suitcase were heavy. I stood dejectedly in front of the horrid looking building on what I deemed a horrid street. The gate was locked, no buzzers or doorbells. Two men and a dog were sitting across the street watching me, and finally one of the men came over to ask if I was looking for accommodations.

"This is the address of the *casa particular* that I booked, but I have no idea how to get in."

He had a kind face that reminded me of the depressed character in the movie *Sideways* and said he too owned a *casa particular* around the corner and was awaiting an Englishman who was a no show. He pointed to what looked like a well-maintained New York character walk-up. I waited and yelled up to Marta. Nothing. They offered to carry my luggage and show me the available room; it was sparse and far less inviting than the façade of the building. I should know by now that looks can be deceiving.

I chose to try Marta's building one last time before taking the room, hoping for something homier. It was a great relief to see the Hotel Nacional one block down the street from each *casa*; I had my bearings and knew where I was located. Being close to the most prestigious hotel in Havana, I felt better about the neighborhood. The men carried my luggage back and waited with me until we got into the building, along with a visiting family. They knew the owner and kissed their hellos.

I breathed a huge sigh of relief upon entering the apartment and meeting Marta. The place is extremely large, fastidiously clean, and charming in an old fashioned way, with '50s furniture, doilies, and fussy bric-a-brac everywhere. Marta was bubbly and welcoming and immediately invited me for dinner that night. I quickly declined, unsure of why. She insisted.

"I will not have you spending Christmas alone!"

I'd forgotten it was Christmas Eve. She was cooking a large turkey, rice and beans, potatoes, salad, and dessert. Her mother and father would be coming, as would two Norwegian women who were staying at the *casa*.

There is a television in my room, so I rested for a while and watched a silly American movie, then went out to investigate the neighborhood. I ate a late lunch in a corner bar just a couple of blocks from the *casa*. Only a few Cubans and two young, bored looking tourists patronized the bar. One of the tourists was uncomfortably overweight, and the other had a dull, glazed look; not the types to get this party started. On the break, a band member sporting long dreadlocks came to my table. The youngest of the group, a fellow with amazing emerald green eyes, honed in on the conversation. He wanted to learn more English and get the correct pronunciation and meanings; clearly, he was in pursuit of an English-speaking girl. A beautiful black teen with huge dimples joined the class. It buoyed my mood to give them English lessons. The waiter came for a dance when the group started and asked me to return to go clubbing with him. Still, he seemed to think it was appropriate to overcharge me.

Outside the bar, a homely nurse dressed in a white '60s uniform, complete with cap, caught my eye. I noticed that she had hairy, bowed legs as she stood firmly planted, intently sucking on a cigarette. I walked past to get a better look and I saw that she was not a woman, but a man. To each his own.

Marta's father is charming and speaks excellent English; her mother is a fine-boned, smiling woman with translucent skin. Her father worked for the embassy, speaks six languages, and seems to be extremely knowledgeable about almost everything. His Chinese father immigrated to Cuba in 1930 and married a *cubana*. I can only imagine the things this man has seen in his lifetime (and I would love to know). The Norwegians were a boisterous and talkative mother and a silent, odd duck daughter who ate very little. They now live in Spain, and the mother spoke heavily accented Spanish. The turkey was fantastic, marinated in garlic and the juice of a weird type of green-skinned orange. The entire meal was delicious. Marta and her father insisted that I stuff myself. It was a pleasant surprise to spend Christmas Eve with these kind strangers. Marta is affectionate and warm—she is, without a doubt, an angel placed on my path on this absurd trip. And she is clearly a professional in comparison to Ricardo and Malita. I don't know if Malita told her what happened in Varadero, but she has been kissing and hugging me as though I were a child, so I assume so.

I tried to nap, to no avail, before heading to Old Havana for my rendezvous. My taxi driver pointed out how quiet the streets were.

"This is not normal. At Christmas, the streets are usually filled with people and the atmosphere is festive and happy. This is eerie. People are afraid right now and unsure of what will happen. It makes me nervous."

Taberna de la Muralla was filled with noisy patrons, and the same house band played. The lead singer who'd asked me to go dancing in September smiled and lit up with recognition, obviously not offended that I'd been a no show. I took the only available table, which was inside, and sat nervously awaiting the French people. I was uncomfortable in my low-cut dancing top, all dressed up and alone on Christmas Eve in Havana, Cuba. I sat for ten minutes as the waiters walked by ignoring me, so that I felt even sillier. A man walked by and asked me, in heavily German-accented Spanish, where I am from. His friend then feigned a trip to the bathroom, clearly appraising me. Shortly thereafter they invited me to join them for a drink. I told them I was meeting a French family, but would join them for the time being.

They were not German, but Austrian. Werner is in the army and works for NATO and is obviously high ranking. He is a tidy, physically fit, no nonsense type. Wolfgang is a friendly, but pervy type, speaks less English, and smokes non-stop. He has sharp features with deep wrinkles (and actually looks like a wolf). I say pervy because of his tales of escapades with young Cuban girls. He told me a story about the night he and a friend were hooked up with a couple of young *cubanas*. They were sitting with two Canadian men who lived part-time in Cuba and smuggled cigars for a living. As they left, one mumbled in Wolfgang's ear, "Be careful. It's a man," nodding to his friend's girl. He warned his friend when the "girl" went to the bathroom.

"No! I know women. She kisses great."

His friend discovered later that night that "she" was, in fact, a man, and Wolfgang found this hilarious. Werner seemed to find his friend's exploits totally distasteful and made it clear that he did not participate in such activities.

I realized I'd been stood up.`

"Typical. No surprise. They are French," Werner said with a scowl.

Is this true? Are the French famous for no shows, or was the comment just a case of Austrian-French rivalry?

My singer grabbed me to dance twice and cameras flashed; I enjoy attention, but not the spotlight. The second time he made up a song with Spanish lyrics crafted to convince me to go out with him. Even though I was sitting with two men, he wasn't about to give up.

I stayed with the Austrians until closing and was relieved to find that they were staying at the Hotel Nacional, so close to my *casa*. This was serendipity at work. The idea of walking alone at night to the taxi stand in Paulo Territory was unnerving.

When I arrived at the apartment, it was late. The old cage style elevator was scary-movie creepy, but even worse, I got to my floor and found a gate locked directly in front of the elevator doors. I didn't know which of the keys to use. I fumbled, afraid to drop them down the shaft. The door opened and closed on me and I hyperventilated for a minute or two, wondering if I'd get trapped in the small space between the doors and the gate. Finally, I found the right key, then yet a fourth key to get into the *casa*, and a fifth for my room. I was sick all night with plugged sinuses from Wolfgang's incessant smoking.

In the morning I asked Marta if I could have breakfast in the *casa*.

"*Si, si,* sit down!"

She graced me with my best breakfast in Cuba so far, with real bread and delicious cheese, grapes, papaya, pineapple, banana, and excellent espresso with hot milk. The bananas taste fantastic here. I said a silent prayer of thanks for the flavorsome food and the hen-clucking care of this lovely woman. Unfortunately, I cannot stay because an Italian, who arrives tomorrow, has booked my room. Malita did not tell me this, probably because Marta's friend has an available *casa* around the corner. I went to look at it and don't like it much. I tried to find a hotel in Old Havana today, but with no luck.

The Austrians invited me to join them at the pool today, but I'm not a poolside girl. I stopped in only to see if they would care to join me this evening at La Dominica for an Italian meal in Habana Vieja. On my way through the lobby, I spotted the expressionless Overstuffed and Dullard from the corner bar wandering around aimlessly. Clearly, they have money (the Hotel Nacional doesn't come cheap), but a lack of imagination about what to do with it.

Werner invited me to join them for a cappuccino, and we got into a fascinating conversation about his work. He has exactly the type of unyielding personality I would expect of an Austrian in the militia, but is interesting and talkative nonetheless. I told him about the fluff movie *Holiday* that I'd seen before I left. It was about swapping homes in different countries, and he thought that to be an excellent idea for us to consider. He would love to ski in the Canadian Rockies and is posted in Hamburg. Unfortunately, I have no desire to go there. They asked why I'd never been to Germany or Austria. I have no interest in the culture, but I laughed and said it was because I would look too common there and I prefer to go where I am considered a little more exotic. That is, in part, the truth.

I walked the Malecón to Old Havana, about a forty-five minute fast-paced jaunt. For the shade, I chose the side of the street with the buildings rather than the side closer to the sea. The hot decay and stench coming from God knows where was almost more than I could handle, and I gagged at one point. Small children played in the doorways of the decrepit buildings.

Two toy trucks that I had in my gift cache were stuffed into my daypack to give away today, and I came across two little boys with their father at a crosswalk.

"Would it be okay if I gave your boys each a truck?" I asked in Spanish.

The father eyed me suspiciously.

"They were gifts for some friends, but I will not be seeing them now."

He hesitated, then reluctantly agreed. The boys looked at me oddly, took the trucks, and walked away. A European couple watched this exchange, and I felt like a stupid tourist afterwards; I knew better than to do this, but wanted to give the toys to someone. I will not give the rest away in such a manner again.

I came across a starving, teeny tiny puppy, with almost hairless skin covered in flakes, scrounging and stumbling around the boulevard. I was annoyed with myself for not bringing my dog treats—this little fellow would have eaten anything. What can one do? It made my heart ache; I weep as I write this, visualizing this innocent little creature all alone and starving to death. Sometimes I cannot bear the reality of life on this planet.

Afraid I would encounter Paulo, I tremulously entered Old Havana. I walked down Obispo to the neighborhood where

Alejandro lives, on the far-fetched chance that I would see him. Even though he is married, he is a friendly face. I sat for a long while, still nervous and woozy from the heat, and took the opportunity to people-watch on the busiest street in Habana Vieja. An amiable old man sat next to me and struck up a conversation. I inquired at a few of the hotels about accommodation, but was still light-headed, so went up to Ambos Mundos to write and catch a breeze.

Dark clouds threatened overhead, and thunder rumbled on my stroll afterward. I was too late to get to the cab area; people lined up there once the deluge started. I had to tuck myself against a building to escape the downpour.

By the time I got to the *casa*, I was ravenous, and Marta agreed to make me a turkey sandwich. I learned she has been married three times. Multiple marriages are commonplace here. She said, as others have, that it is cheap, quick, and easy to divorce in Cuba. She also informed me that there is no need to worry that an ex-spouse will take half of your home. What's yours is yours. She lived and worked in Czechoslovakia for five years and was able to do so because of her father's high placement in the embassy. She is a journalist, but said, "The pay is boolshit." Here was another journalist speaking the same sentiments as Paulo. It was a little ironic.

That evening, the Austrians were thrilled with our meal and said it was the best they'd had on their whole trip. Unfortunately, the rain was unremitting, so we had to dine inside, and the restaurant was filled with chain-smoking Europeans. I was agape as one French woman blew clouds of smoke all over her food, eating and smoking at the same time. *Je ne comprend pas.*

We walked to Taberna de la Muralla for an after-dinner drink. Werner leaves in the morning and was surprisingly disappointed to be going home. Last night he said he would not be returning to Cuba and disliked it, but after the nice dinner and good music at the bar, he changed his tune. He even loosened up and bought a CD from one of the groups, after I'd purchased one at the restaurant earlier. Wolfgang was quite taken with me last night, but today he was silent—no loss.

A highly nontraditional Christmas day, *non?*

December 26th

The ocean was choppy today, with high waves crashing over the seawall and onto the walkway. It is overcast and cooler. I am at the Ambos Mundos again, after another long walk along the Malecón and through Old Havana.

This morning I moved to the gloomy room. I am staying with a less than cheery woman named Consuela and her eighty-nine year old mother. The consolation is that the apartment faces the ocean and the Hotel Nacional. Consuela called Marta's this morning to ask if I could come quickly, so that I could get my things in the room and then leave for the fumigation. Aren't you supposed to be out of a building for two days after fumigation? Here is something else to add to the inescapable smoking and heavy pollution of Havana.

A well-muscled, handsome Dane (who looked like a tattooed caricature of a sailor) was clearing out of one of the rooms, and said that he'd been well taken care of and that they had helped him with some passport problems.

Marta made me a fantastic farewell breakfast before I left: a fluffy, soft cheese omelet, much better than at home, fruit, bread and her wonderful *café con leche*. I could fatten up quickly under her roof. She is chubby and her two boys, with their full cheeks, remind me of Alvin and the Chipmunks.

She kissed and hugged me again this morning. "*¡Hay* (pronounced "I") *Mami!*" she always says, holding my face and shaking her head, and I now know she knows about Paulo. She tut-tuts and says she is sorry, but doesn't ask questions or mention the "international incident." I wish I could remain there under her protective wing.

I've searched for a room for Darshana's arrival and bypassed the obvious—the Ambos Mundos. I now have an outrageously expensive reservation and was able to send an email to my mum from the lobby computer to tell her about my change in plans. The rooms are not impressive, but the location is great. I want Dar to enjoy all of my finds in the luxury of Old Havana without the hassle of commuting back and forth to Vedado. This moving around is for the birds.

I went back to the same spot on the Prado, with food this time, and searched for the starving puppy on the boulevard and park across the street, but I had no luck. Silly, I know. What were the chances of finding him in the hustle and bustle of this city?

Old Havana was extremely quiet last night, but is teeming with tourists today. It makes me more obscure in the crowds. I half expect to see Paulo walking down the street, tugging on the hand of another blonde foreigner, a new victim in tow. The International Film Festival is starting with some kind of celebration, but nobody knows when or where. Carrie and Gaby have arrived from Canada, and I called Carrie's *casa* to see if they will be going to the Jazz Café, but there was no answer. If I can't reach them, I may be stuck in that old *casa* in Vedado tonight. I have no plans and no ideas. I am restless, so I will go for another walk along Obispo and then head back to Vedado. I had another terrible sleep last night. A nap is in order.

Wonders never cease. I sat on Obispo to rest, people-watch, and again, see if by some stroke of luck, Alejandro would walk by.

Within ten minutes, he did. He almost fell over when he saw me.

He is not an overly attractive man, but has great energy and intelligence. He also dresses with panache; I assume it is due to the influence of his world travel.

He'd called Marta's number this morning, but the young boy said I'd moved and did not give him Consuela's number. He looked around nervously then asked me to meet him at the bar down the street in ten minutes.

"La Lluvia de Oro?" I guessed.

"*Si.*"

Ten minutes later, he waved hello to the band and walked over.

"Go to snowy door across from shoe store on Obrapia. I will be waiting for you in the door," he whispered clandestinely in his broken English.

Inside the entrance sat the beloved shepherd he had told me about. I whispered his name and he responded. So this was *his* house? Alejandro came in quietly, took me down a long hall, pulled me into a sparse room, then grabbed me and kissed me deeply as though we were long lost lovers. I sputtered.

"Where are we? Your house?"

"No, my house is upstairs. This is the house of my good friend."

Same difference. He leaned in to kiss me again and I pulled away.

"My wife will not be home for two hours," he whispered nervously. He jumped with every sound.

"Look, I will not do this."

"Why not?"

"Are you kidding? It's ridiculous. I've had one bad experience and do not need another."

He asked what had happened and I gave him few details, to which he responded, "Be bery careful who you associate with in Cuba."

Would I visit the gallery of a famous artist back on Obispo and see what I thought of the work?

"I want to export his art to Canada. And then I can come to see you!" he said with a big smile, holding my face in his hands.

"Can I come to your *casa* to visit you?"

Did "visit" mean have sex?

"No. I am staying with two older women."

"It should be fine. It's permitted at *casas* here."

I'll say. The whole of Cuba is fucking itself senseless. He went up to his *casa* first and then I left, feeling strange and unsettled.

I stopped in at Café Paris, a little bar mentioned in one of my books. An unusually insipid trio played. A European woman ripped apart half a fried chicken with gusto and was inhaling it, so I ordered the same; however, I cut into mine and it was pink with blood.

The line-up was coiled out the door and down the street at the Chocolate Museum, but a nearby *pastelería* had some wonderful flan to quell the queasiness of the chicken experience. Yet another woman, who had a long story and was looking for money, accosted me. It has been an unvarying theme of this trip.

I am uneasy about the meeting with Alejandro. It was seamy, and I can't help but feel duplicitous.

The high wind along the Malecón whipped my hair into knots, and a light rain began, so I grabbed a taxi. Back at the *casa*, I felt even seedier. The apartment has not been painted in many years and the ratty furniture is dismal. I left a message at both Carrie's and Gaby's, anxious for their company.

I opened the bedding to take a nap and saw that the sheets had not been changed. The pillowcases smelled of someone's dirty hair, and my spirits sank. A wave of depression washed over me.

I lay down on the other end of the bed and collapsed, staring off into space for a long while.

Should I just leave?

And go where?

I can't bear to get into this bed.

Will I have to sleep in my clothes on top of the duvet?

Where in the hell am I anyway?

I was immobilized, but couldn't sleep, despite my fatigue. I tried to watch TV to numb my brain, but could only get reception to the three legal propaganda channels. The only reading I could focus on was an old copy of *The Lonely Planet*.

Screw this, I thought. I am concerned about offending the owner, when she did not have the decency to change the sheets? Why should I sleep in someone's dirt? I asked for new bedding, much to her annoyance. The fresh sheets cheered me considerably.

I read that the best *paladar* (privately owned restaurant) in all of Havana was only a few blocks from the *casa*, so made a plan to find it. I reluctantly got ready and discovered the tiny door of the restaurant on a dark and dusty side street, minus any signage. I knocked, and a woman opened the peephole and then escorted me past the tables to a tiny, freezer-level, air-conditioned waiting room, with cabinets full of liquors and wines at the back. Old mafia movies flitted through my mind.

I waited. And waited. A man came in to reshelve a bottle of rum.

"Why am I in here?" I asked. *Freezing my ass off in this meat locker*, I wanted to say.

I will climb a mountain for the chance of an excellent meal, so I waited it out in the cooler. Finally, the owner returned and seated me in a tiny room with only three tables, one empty and another with a girl dining alone. The government limits seating in private restaurants so that they will not compete with the state restaurants. I ordered the specialty mentioned in the book, *La*

Guajira, a traditional dish of pork steak, rice and black beans, a *tamal*, fried green plantains, and something called *malanga*.

It was good food, but once again, the bill was padded. Do they think that we pull our dollars off of trees? That we do not work for our money? It must be an art to feign surprise when questioned about a bill.

Right now, this feels like a society that feeds parasitically, without limit or compunction, on its very livelihood.

December 27th

I lit candles in the room last night, and with the sunflowers I'd bought from an old man in Cuban pesos, the room was cheerier. I slept better than any night here, because my room has two windows, so that fresh air cools it. I awoke early to a downpour, but gradually fell back to sleep, in spite of the horrendous traffic.

My laptop was recharging in the living room, because of the antiquated sockets in my room. To my surprise, the living room was being painted a lovely warm yellow by two men. Another unexpected surprise: a shower with hot water and full pressure. As soon as I finished, a smiling man named Rolando popped out of the kitchen to offer me breakfast. He set a beautiful table with fresh fruit, *café con leche*, fresh bread, cheeses, and scrambled eggs done with tomatoes, chard, and onions. Although I prefer the autonomy of hotels, in Cuba it is in the *casas particulares* where one is well fed. I asked if he was family, but no, Consuela has a maid-man, as I used to back home.

Her quick-witted mother came out of her room to say hello and discuss the bad weather. The large apartment has tremendous potential. There is a wall-to-wall window with wide, white wooden shutters leading to a large patio and, as I mentioned, a view of the sea and the Hotel Nacional. With the first coat of paint, already the place looks much improved.

Consuela told me that Alejandro had called to apologize. He would be unable to meet me, because he had to get medicine for his mother. It was just as well. I had no intention of having him visit the home of these two women.

I asked to borrow an umbrella, but the rain slowed to a mist, so I could walk to Habana Vieja. Rita was right—she predicted that I would hate the tremendous car pollution, saying that she'd had enough of it in a couple of days. Staying outside of the old town, I find that the fumes are overwhelming. My throat is raw from walking. I tried to escape by moving to the quieter street paralleling the Malecón, but it was much the same.

In this tourist-free area, nobody paid me any mind. I was fascinated with the decrepitude and antiquity of the buildings. I stopped numerous times to stare at the Neoclassical, Renaissance, and Baroque architecture, trying to imagine this city in its earlier splendor, with horse-drawn carriages and people dressed in their finery on the many romantic wrought iron balconies. I also tried to visualize what it would look like if a grand scale restoration were to be implemented throughout the entire city.

This city is an old, old man with deeply etched wrinkles, gnarled limbs and callosity, sweaty and unshaven—all evidence of a long, harsh existence. My city is a newborn baby by comparison, fresh and free from blemishes, and without history.

A momentary wave of panic hit with the nightmarish image of what this city would be like in the midst of a *revolución*, with power out, food and water unavailable, and chaos reigning. I envisioned the days of the Black Plague in old London, with rats running in packs through the streets, and the decay of the city finally overwhelming its inhabitants (and guests).

Talk about *merde!* One must be constantly vigilant not to step in the soft turds that litter the narrow sidewalks.

As I entered Old Havana, a man passed by and tried to say, as clearly as possible in English, "I love you."

I laughed loudly because of his articulation, and he followed me down the street. I've discovered the trick is not to say, "I have a boyfriend"—they don't care about a man across an ocean. "*Yo tengo un novio cubano*" (I have a Cuban boyfriend), said with conviction, will usually get me off the hook.

"Ahhhhhh," they say with a shrug and a nod that denotes respect, and off they go.

Unbefuckinglievable.

It was too cold to keep writing in the wind, so I left the rooftop terrace to have lunch elsewhere. I was almost right—it was not a foreigner, but there on Obispo was Paulo, sauntering arm in arm down the street with a *cubana* in an intimate little conversation. I halted in my tracks, my jaw dropped, and my heart pounded as I watched the lovebirds pass by. There is no way he did not see me; he is far too hawk-like. He was glacier cool, strolling nonchalantly past me, pretending to be much too fascinated in what she was saying to notice me. I was on the verge of running after them in a knee-jerk reaction, wanting to say, "Hello! Did you know Paulo came to Varadero to sleep with me and convince me to marry him? Did he tell you that he had a Canadian girlfriend?"

She would most likely speak no English, and I am sure my Spanish would desert me under duress. I stood fixed to the spot. If I were to jeopardize whatever he is getting from her, he would surely be infuriated, and who knows what he would do? At this moment, I would love to make his life miserable, but I don't need to ruin hers. He is probably already doing a good job of that. I watched them waltz down the street and then I walked off to La Dominica in a fog. I didn't taste the meal and could focus only on eating quickly and leaving. As if to punctuate the whole rotten scene, my bill had a 100 percent tip added. How perfectly appropriate.

I have no one to talk to, and it frustrates me to no end, so I came back to the Ambos Mundos lobby to spew my thoughts out of my mind and onto this page. I cannot wait for Darshana to arrive tomorrow. I am tired of carrying this garbage around in my head. The words—the insults—are flying through my brain. I want to tell Paulo what an A plus ass he is, what a degenerate-*jinetero* he is, he who calls everyone else low class. I want to write his mother to tell her what a swine she raised.

I am infuriated.

I am fed up with this lousy trip.

I want to scream.

I feel claustrophobic.

He will now be on a stalking mission in Old Havana; I am sure of it. Thank God I am in Vedado tonight and will be with Dar when I stay on his terrain for the next two days. I wonder if he has called Ricardo to rant for telling him I returned to Canada.

I am reeling.

I took the first taxi I could find back from Old Havana. It was a run-down, beaten-up, illegal Lada taxi and I thought it would break down along the way. I have showered and am awaiting Carrie's call to let me know when her group is leaving for the Jazz Café.

In the late afternoon, I came to get more clothes for a long walk around Vedado to walk my mind into exhaustion. *Abuela* gave me a warm hug, but Consuela seems only to tolerate guests as a means to an end. I can't blame her. I can imagine the hassle of running a Cuban *casa particular*, with an endless stream of foreigners doing God knows what under one's roof.

I walked far off into the heart of the neighborhood, passing a lively outdoor market, nice single dwelling homes, and some points of interest, then back along the Malecón. This segment of the seawall was eerily quiet, with no vehicular traffic and only a few people walking about. I passed many police on the opposite side of the street. At one of the police kiosks, an officer asked me to cross the street. Because I am who I am, I questioned him—a communist police officer in a foreign country.

"*¿Porque?*" I asked.

"*¿Porque?*" he repeated incredulously.

"I'm only curious," I said.

He obliged and said that I must cross because I was in the territory of the US Embassy. His explanation made no sense to me. As I walked further along, I came across a huge red billboard with a picture of George Bush that had a plus sign, and a picture of another political figure I don't recognize (but must research), and then an equal sign and a picture of Adolf Hitler, bright red painted in the pupils of his eyes.

Further on, I came across what seemed like one hundred black flags with a star in the center flying in front of a building. Near the flags was a sign that read *Patria o Muerte*—Homeland or Death. On the boardwalk was another huge billboard of Bush with red fire in his eyes, vampire teeth dripping with blood, and a bloodied hand and gun beside him. By the image of Bush, "The Assassin" was written, in Spanish. I can't really argue the point, but the whole scene was disturbing. Off the beaten path, you get a sense of the real political climate. This is no joke. I looked for information in a guidebook and discovered that the building is, in fact, the de facto US Embassy, but I still do not understand what the deal is between these two enemies and why it is so heavily guarded.

The Cuban Chronicles

December 28th

I am awaiting Dar's arrival at the Ambos Mundos like a little girl awaiting a playmate. We have an arrangement for 11 a.m., but if she doesn't make an early bus, we have a back-up plan for 1 p.m. here on the terrace. I have moved to this hotel, and the rooms are disappointingly small and basic. I took advantage of the good shower at Consuela's this morning to scrub the grit, smoke, salt, and pollution out of my hair and had another decent breakfast.

At the end of my unnerving walk last night, I went to the *paladar* to book a reservation for Dar and me. I stopped at the corner bar for a drink and then got ready for the evening. The Jazz Café was surprisingly sans ambience. I expected it to be a traditional Cuban bar, but it was chrome '80s modern with no charm.

Carrie is a tall, slender woman with unruly curls who looks much younger than her thirty-five years. She is the friend who had the Cuban musician home-stay with her and subsequently bore his child. We discussed her situation; she has brought Lola, who is now ten months old, to Cuba. I asked if the father knew she was coming, and she said he did not. She was jittery and watchful while he walked around the bar pre-performance, and I asked her what she expected to gain from the surprise appearance. She hopes that he will be interested in meeting Lola. She wants to be able to tell her daughter that she met her father and had been in his country. She wants pictures for Lola's future queries and she wants him to acknowledge his daughter's existence. Carrie knows that Alvar has a wife and child here and that he loves them and loves Cuba. She is by no means stupid, but wants to offer some semblance of a history to her daughter and is optimistic that he will be open to a meeting.

Gaby is another tall and trim woman. Her youthful looking in-laws joined us. Her new Cuban husband arrived in Canada only in September, and did not return with her to Havana for the Christmas salsa tour Gaby is hosting. I wonder what he thought of his first white Christmas. I know he is having a hard time adjusting to our North American diet and fell ill when he arrived, due to the drastic climate change.

The band was what I assume would be considered excellent, although I have no knowledge of jazz and little interest in it. Midway through the set, the bar's air conditioning kicked in full blast, much to everyone's dismay. It was cool yesterday anyway. Even the men were complaining and shivering. My sore throat got worse by the minute and I impatiently waited for the band to stop, curious about Alvar's reaction upon seeing Carrie. He was definitely surprised, but seemed pleased. I hope he will meet Lola so she has memories of her father, unlike you. As you know, it is a longing that remains with you for all time, and the problem is even more difficult when your father resides in another country.

A table of four handsome young men sat in front of our table, and one, who was shivering, wrapped himself in his jacket, which had French written on it. Judging by their dark, swarthy looks and their mannerisms, my guess was that they were from France, not Québec. When the band quit, I asked one if he spoke English.

"A leetle."

"Hand over the jacket!" I said, miming a gun.

Laughing, *"Mais, non!"*

"France?" I asked.

"Oui."

He was eager to converse and to make plans. Age seems to be no issue at all with young Frenchmen, as you've said in your many letters from Paris. He is here until April, learning Cuban salsa, because he intends to open a studio in Paris. When I left, he invited me to meet his group today at a rumba concert somewhere, but for the life of me, I cannot remember the name of the place.

I shared a taxi with a Canadian who was part of Gaby's tour group.

"El Presidente! Lamparilla! El Presidente! Lamparilla!" he kept shouting the street names at the driver as though the man was deaf or stupid, his Spanish an assault to the ears. He was clearly terrified of getting lost, poor fellow.

After we dropped him off (you know, on the corner of El Presidente and Lamparilla), the driver whipped around, waving his hands.

"Hee's crazy! Es he your friend?"

"No, I just met him tonight with friends," I giggled.

"He keeps yelling El Presidente! Lamparilla! You sure he es not crazy?"

Nope. He was just the quintessential fledgling tourist.

I tossed and turned the night away with obsessive thoughts of all of the nasty things I would like to say to Paulo.

Darshana did not show for our 11 a.m. appointment, and I hope she arrives at 1 p.m. If not, I have this ridiculously expensive room for no reason and I don't know what I will do with the rest of the day; I've had my hopes set on giving her a tour of Habana Vieja. I went to the bank to get cash; nobody wants credit cards, even in this big hotel. After leaving one bank that was lined up a hundred people deep, I went to another, but they would not take my traveler's cheques, and the commission for a Visa advance was astronomical. The hotel will not exchange the cheques either. It is quite the system.

I will rest and meditate while I await my rendezvous. I will pray.

I am ready to shove every cigar I smell up each smoking man's ass in this hotel lobby right now. Does that cover my mood? How can one trip here be so wonderful, and the next one so bad? I have tried to make the best of it, but the truth of the matter is that I am miserable. Dar is a no show. Unless she has broken a leg, I don't know what excuse is acceptable. Through my sister, she knows that I've had problems with Paulo. I reconfirmed our plans twice from here. We discussed it before I left so there would be absolutely no confusion or misunderstandings. I have awaited her arrival date since the beginning of the trip, excited to show her all my finds, to go dancing, and to be with a friend. I have the reservation at the little *paladar* in Vedado; I'm not going to take a taxi back and forth, when I could have walked to the restaurant had I stayed on at Consuela's.

The last time I wanted to go home early from a holiday, I was nineteen years old, in the dead of winter in drab, damp old England, suffering with near-pneumonia, but never again until now.

My motto, like the bumper sticker about fishing, is that a bad day of traveling is better than any day at work. I long ago sacrificed my house and the luxury of living "normally;" instead I have lived in my "student" apartment, so that I have as many opportunities as possible to travel. I didn't think it was possible to feel this way doing my favorite thing in life. I have been unable to escape the dark cloud of Paulo.

I had to go to yet another bank and stand in the queue for over an hour. Afterward, the music and the band's friendly banter at Lluvia de Oro lightened my somber mood. I wanted to get drunk, but as is the way with me, any more than one drink at a time leaves me with a raging headache. What good is that? My throat is burning from the pollution and I have been fighting traveler's diarrhea since I arrived.

How had Paulo planned to wander Habana Vieja hand in hand with me without being seen by his girlfriend? I guess this is why he so badly wanted to get me out of Havana and go to Cienfuegos, Pinales, Pinar del Río, and Trinidad. And how would he have managed it if I'd asked him to go snore at home? No wonder he wanted to ensure I would spend 24/7 with him. Let me tell you, little Miguel is looking like a superhero with a cape right now.

My Costco case pack of condoms is still untouched, lying dormant at the bottom of my suitcase. What did I think this would be? A fucking parade?

A uniformed schoolgirl and her father were sitting on the couch next to me in the lobby, animatedly chatting. Fed up, and in spite of the fact that the father lit a cigarette earlier, I asked him, "Does *everyone* in Cuba smoke?"

"Yes, I am afraid so."

He introduced himself and began a long conversation. He is allegedly a professor of design at the university. He offered his email address and asked for mine. I couldn't resist; he was too handsome and well spoken.

I have to admit, it is a nice change to be situated in this busy, central hotel and watch the activities in the ambient lobby bar, while conversing with different people from all over the world. And my room is right down the hall from #511—Hemingway's.

December 29th

I sat in the lobby of the hotel until I got bored. I had no idea what to do for the evening and hoped a cool shower would wash away my irritation and bring me inspiration. The phone rang as I entered the room. I assumed it was the reception desk to tell me the Internet was up and running again. I was shocked to hear Handsome Lobby

Guy, Javier, on the other end of the line. He said he did not know if I was a guest of the hotel, but decided to take a chance.

"You must be well known at the hotel, because they knew whom I was speaking about immediately."

"Maybe it's all of that hanging out in the lobby."

"I don't know … I felt something talking with you, so I decided I must call the hotel."

"Yes," I wanted to say, "That is the hopeful wellspring of *I sense an escape from Cuba.*"

Of course, I said no such thing.

Did I want to go out with him tonight? Why not? Maybe it would pull me out of this dark blue funk over Dar's no-show. I suggested the usual Taberna de la Muralla.

I spot him sitting expectantly at an outdoor table. The night is balmy and pleasant. His hair is gelled, and he looks and smells freshly showered (apparently water is about ten cents a month, so there are no problems with hygiene in this country). He is dressed conservatively, and I notice his highly polished, academic looking shoes. He is intelligent and has an engaging manner, but the conversation is vaguely reminiscent of Paulo's frustration and anger with the system, especially over the wages of professionals. As a professor with a Master's degree, he earns the equivalent of $35 US a month. The fact that waiters earn more than professionals is clearly a huge bone of contention—understandably so—and he displays a similar level of bitterness and pedantic railing to Paulo's. Castro, it seems, made a grave error in running two currencies. Anyone in tourism has access to the CUC, while the highly educated professionals must live with the paltry Cuban peso.

He comments that I am not revealing much of myself. I tell him I've had a problem with a Cuban man, and so I am guarded.

He wants to know what happened, but I don't give details. He sings me the national anthem: he says he is different, not like other Cuban men, et cetera, et cetera.

Uh huh.

He says I have poured cold water all over his romantic mood and aspirations with my story of the Cuban man and with my cool reserve.

Qué lástima (too bad), I think.

He draws an engineer's map of his *casa*. He has the impeccable printing of a graphic designer. He lives in his own home, with an aunt living in a separate section. His ten-year-old daughter lives with her mother, and they were apparently never married. He says he has never been married. I find that hard to believe and I say so.

He tells me he and his daughter watched me today as I furiously pounded on my laptop. They were trying to figure out what I could be writing, and speculating about who I was and what I did. His daughter snuck a peek at my screen and told her father I was writing in English. He told her that it was impolite to look, but he was secretly as curious as she. I had not noticed any of this, as I had been completely shrouded in my own little bitch cloud. When I spoke to him, his daughter encouraged it. Her mother came by to pick up her daughter while we were exchanging addresses.

He tells me a good friend of his is a *babalao* (meaning, literally, father of the secrets), a Santería priest, who only two days before had told him he would meet a blonde woman who would be important in his life. He says that although he is a pragmatic engineer, he now believes.

I ask him about the US Embassy and the large billboard with the second man depicted with Bush and Hitler. He is Luis Posada Carriles, considered a Cuban traitor. He explains the story.

"Why are we speaking of politics? Why not of us?"

"Maybe I'm a spy."

"Maybe you are."

He suggests that we leave and—lo and behold—he pays the bill. Maybe I should give him a medal of honor.

We walk the Malecón and we stop to sit on the seawall in front of a cruise ship, an uncommon sight. Few cruise ships stop here because of the American law that forbids any ship that has docked in Cuba to dock in the United States of America for six months. It is actually a saving grace for the already failing environmental health of the area.

He tries to draw more information out of me, in the way you would with someone you were trying to engage in a future relationship. He tells me about his career and his time spent working in Spain, Germany, and Italy. He says he seriously contemplated defecting to Spain, but was afraid of living in complete destitution in a foreign country that has no programs for refugees. He explains the *bombo* lottery and how he has long hoped he will win entrance into the USA. The lottery is a special Cuban migration program that is reviewed each year for its terms and number of entrants. We speak of our interests and discover that we both paint. He says he likes to paint figurative work, but cannot afford the materials. Always, these men speak of *la lucha*, the struggle.

He leans in and attempts to kiss me. I could not be less interested. My usually easy-to-arouse lips are numb and neutralized by the bull of these men. Because of my reticence, he suggests I tell him how I like to be kissed.

"Better still, show me."

I don't know why, but I find this hysterically funny and can't stop laughing. Slightly offended, and realizing he is getting nowhere fast, he suggests we walk. We look for a *tienda* to buy a bottle of water, then sit in the Plaza de Armas close to the hotel. A group is singing and playing guitar in the park, and he explains what the beautiful sounding songs mean, and how they are considered subversive. Although I am in a jaded mood, I am enjoying his company.

A dog meanders by scavenging for food, and I pull out my dog treats. He asks what they are. I am astonished that his response is the same, almost verbatim, to Paulo's. Actually, his mannerisms and sentiments are unnervingly the same. It could be the mannerisms and expressions of this group or class; I don't know. It is almost four in the morning when we get to the hotel.

"When will I see you again?" he asks at the doorway of the hotel.

A sleepy guard awakens to let me in. I say I will call him. I notice two Cubans on the Internet in the dark and ask them how they got online, since I've had such difficulties. With a card, they say, and I am sure the guard has let them in to use the computers illegally. All of this is so Orwellian that I am glad they have grabbed one piece of freedom, albeit in the middle of the night.

I have just fallen asleep when I hear the knob of my door rattling, as someone tries to get in my room. I scream out and hear the footsteps of someone running down the hall and down the stairs. Heart racing, I get up to use the washroom and find I have run out of toilet paper and must use the crisp "sanitized" paper band that was wrapped around the toilet. For this price they couldn't spare a square? I decide I will leave to find a *casa particular* in the morning.

Eight
Sleepless in Havana

© Wanda St.Hilaire

His designs were strictly honorable, as the phrase is; that is, to rob a woman of her fortune by way of marriage.
—Henry Fielding
English Novelist and Dramatist
(*Tom Jones*)

December 30th

Yesterday I awakened far too early and could not get back to sleep. That dizzy, uncoordinated sensation that comes with sleep deprivation has overtaken me. Each night I go to bed late and cannot sleep, with events, faces, and places swirling in my mind, all so foreign, and then I awaken early to the same thoughts and images.

I showered and then called Marta to see if, by some chance, the Norwegians had left.

"You are a lucky girl. They decided to go to Varadero today."

"I'll be there in an hour."

I went up to the terrace for a tasteless breakfast and packed at the speed of light. When I arrived, Elena and Marta were scrubbing the apartment down in their morning ritual, and my new room was ready.

I desperately needed more sleep and asked for a wake up call for the walk back to the Ambos Mundos for my 1 p.m. meeting with Anna. She and her sister and two friends arrived from Montreal last night. Surely *she* will show, I thought, as I went unconscious.

Elena tried to wake me, but I could not lift my head off the pillow. I woke late; tried to do something with my puffy, sleep-creased, not-so-pretty face; and grabbed a taxi. My driver was the same one I got the day I moved to the Ambos Mundos. He owns an immaculate, air-conditioned Peugeot and is a friendly, smiling man. We negotiated a fare back to Varadero for my flight home.

I sat and waited for Anna at the elevator chairs near the entrance of the terrace, to avoid the huge European tour group who were smoking themselves into a frenzy. I sat dejectedly as the clock ticked closer and closer to 1:30. Just at the moment I was about to give up and leave, Anna and her sister Catarina rushed off of the elevator. I practically leapt on them.

We sat over a drink on the patio, Anna itching to hear what had transpired so far. Remember: aside from you in Paris, she'd been my closest confidante on the Paulo affair, having helped translate his letters. She had not received my Cuban email telling her that Paulo and I were through on the first day. She'd called his sister's house upon arrival, to ask if he was there and if we were together, but had only received a reluctant "I don't know." I hesitated to tell the real story; I couldn't read her sister, whom I'd only met for the first time, and I was uncomfortable sharing the sordid details. Anna urged me to tell all, and with the events bottled up and no verbal outlet, I let it spill out everywhere.

"I am glad that we are now in Havana and we can all be together. I am happy to see you, my friend. You must stay in Havana until your flight leaves and spend New Year's Eve with us," Anna stated.

Next, it was their turn. They launched into their own bizarre story. The evening before, they'd gone out to a small nightclub in Habana Vieja at the posh Hotel Florida. A group of young Rastafarians fraternized with them, and one had a British girlfriend who was sixty years old. In spite of the age difference, the girls thought the couple looked good together. When the bar closed at two in the morning, they went out into the street, with three Rastas following and pitching the idea to go to another bar. Anna said she did not want to drink any more and was ready to go home. The men were persistent, but Anna and Catarina walked off, shouting a farewell.

Alerted by the girls' forceful good-bye, police on a nearby corner came over and asked the men for identification. Within minutes, police swarmed the street and arrested two of the Rastas. The third quickly exited down an alleyway with their friend Nana, escaping the police. My friends tried to explain that there was no problem. Anna speaks fluent Spanish, so there was no language barrier, but the police told them that as far as they were concerned, the men were harassing tourists. The British woman stood by silently, unable to speak Spanish, even though one of the men being arrested was her boyfriend.

Anna could see the frustration, the hatred, and the feelings of being subjected to gross injustice in the eyes of the two Rastas. The bigotry of the police and their smug sense of supremacy was palpable. Again, the girls pleaded, but the police took the two men away handcuffed.

The third Rasta and Nana appeared from the darkened alleyway. He told them the seriousness of the situation and that his friends could be in jail for a long time. The only way out was for Catarina and Anna to go to the police station and say that the men were their boyfriends. The girls felt guilty for having caused the arrest and were unsure what to do. Was this a set-up? Feeling responsible, they reluctantly agreed. They walked down the deserted, decrepit streets, hoping like hell that they were not being led into a trap. Finally they arrived at the police station.

"What is this? The Jamaican invasion?" the police joked with sarcasm.

Anna and Catarina explained that they had known these men for some time and that they were, in fact, their boyfriends. After some banter, the police decided to let Catarina's "boyfriend" out, but stubbornly kept Diego, Anna's "boyfriend," in jail.

The situation provoked an unexpected emotional response in Anna, stirring memories of having lived through injustices in third world countries. She was born in the Portuguese colony of Angola and had lived in Peru and Bolivia. Her body and mind recalled past moments of fear and frustration. The idea of Diego being left alone in this dingy prison overwhelmed her. Half playacting the melodramatic Latina girlfriend in a Mexican *novela* and half on the verge of cracking from the tension and hatred between the police and the Rastas, she cried out, *"Mia! Mia! Let mine out too!"*

The scene was so theatrical that the police burst out laughing, and even Diego began laughing. Her operatic display was inspiration enough for the police to release him.

"But didn't you just arrive here last night at 6 p.m.?" I asked.

"Yes," they both answered in unison.

Welcome to Cuba.

We moved to the Lluvia de Oro for live music and lunch. My heart lightened as I danced and laughed with friends. We left too soon, because we had arranged to meet Catarina's two friends at the Plaza de la Catederal.

Karen is small with shoulder-length brown hair. She is thirty-six, but looks no more than twenty-five. I wish. Nana is forty-six, tiny and in good shape with short black hair and sharp, masculine features. I hadn't expected Anna's sister Catarina to be so striking. She is Spanish-looking with wavy, long black hair, large almond eyes, a pretty face, and a voluptuous body. Anna, petite and beautiful as well, downplays her Latina-ness, whereas Catarina accentuates it.

We lingered in the busy square at the large outdoor café, while a more subdued, generic band played in the background. Anna spotted a Santería tarot reader, an enormous black woman dressed in all white, as is typical of the Santerían, with a huge cigar in her mouth. She was surrounded by bizarre paraphernalia, including an orange monkey hanging from a nearby tree. Our curiosity got the best of us. Anna had a reading, Catarina wrote down what was told, and I watched and photographed. The woman did an incantation and then recited a blessing of some type, sprinkling strongly perfumed water on all three of us. She spread out her tarot cards and gruffly read, all the while chewing on the fat stogie. I understood little of her slang Spanish, but enjoyed the weirdness. I was dressed in black. The woman abruptly stopped and turned to me at one point, telling me never to wear all black; instead I must wear something red with black. Lipstick would not suffice; the red item should be made of cloth. Anna translated the reading over a drink, but it was mostly typical, trite mumbo jumbo.

Santería, a religion brought over by African slaves, has a huge influence on the Cuban culture. Some Catholic saints were chosen as deities, called *orishás*, as a mask to hide traditional Yoruba beliefs and to appease slave masters and priests. Everyone responds favorably to Nana's name because she is an important female *orishá* of creation, the sky mother.

The kitchen was warm and full of life while the evening's dinner was being prepared at the girls' *casa* by the owner and her two sous-chefs. To say I was shocked by their accommodations would be an understatement. The dirt streets off the Prado are virtually a ghetto. The humid little house, although clean, is dilapidated and the rooms are sparse and threadbare, with some small racks hanging about as closets. The austerity of the two cramped rooms for the four women is in such stark contrast to the luxury of Anna's home and lifestyle that I was completely taken aback. Although my day-to-day lifestyle is much more basic than hers, I could not stay at this shabby *casita*. The dreariness and dismal surroundings would depress me further than the events so far already have. Remembering my initial reaction to the apartment and neighborhood, I had an instantaneous change of perspective on Marta's *casa* relative to this one. By comparison, I am staying at the Havana Hilton.

While we waited for dinner, Anna and I came up with the bright idea to call Paulo's sister to let her know what her brother was up to these days. I tried to grasp the conversation, but it became one-sided as Anna listened to a long-winded tale on the other end. I found it odd that his sister would share so much information with a complete stranger, and Anna's face indicated it was not a happy story. The family Paulo was living with was not his own, but another, from whom he was renting a room. The woman on the line said Paulo had been warm and friendly and had even taken their children out to the park sometimes. But one day he disappeared, leaving only a few old clothes. He'd been making numerous phone calls, mostly to his mommy in Cienfuegos, but said he had paid the bills. One day a representative of the phone company came to the door with a $1400 peso bill. A typical Cuban family, they were probably earning somewhere around $250 pesos per month, and could not afford such a bill. The woman asked Anna if I would meet with her to go to the police. I do not wish to spend a day at a Cuban police station, nor do I want her asking me to pay the bill out of the goodness of my heart—a highly probable request. I certainly have no inclination to cover a bill that ass racked up.

The dinner was tasty, with a large fresh salad of lettuce and tomato. It was a pleasure, since you can't find a decent salad in a restaurant. It helps the running of the *casa* financially to have its guests dine in. The *casas particulares* are required to pay a heavy tax each month, whether it is high season or low, and whether their rooms are occupied or not. They must report each small purchase and sale with a complicated accounting of everything. I am sure there are ways around the system, but there is no way around the taxes. Alvira, the owner, is a warm and accommodating host. I wonder how she and the other women are taking to Anna's strict and explicit instructions on the cooking of each meal. I'm quite sure Marta would not be as receptive.

Anna and I took a taxi to my place to change for a street party that evening. It was to be held outside the US Embassy under the ominous black flags, and two live bands would be playing. We met up with Catarina, Karen, and Nana, who were already dancing when we arrived. The four women have come to Cuba specifically for a dancing holiday. Catarina and Nana are serious *salseras* and all are taking private rumba and salsa classes each morning at the *casa particular*. It is an intensive, sweaty workout and they've invited me to join in, but the offer holds no appeal. I just don't take dancing that seriously.

Catarina has already hooked up with a warm, conservative looking man named Arturo. They danced beautifully together, and her smile lit up the night. She divulged to me that she came to Cuba with the intention of having her first sexual experience with a black man and it looks as though her wish will be fulfilled.

Immediately, young, dark Cuban men descended on Anna and me, hovering about asking questions. Our North American space and touch boundaries are vastly different to the Cubans', who, on the whole, don't have any. One latched onto me, and his hands were sticky and sweaty on my arm. Another young man with long, wiry dreadlocks honed in more aggressively, crowding Sticky Hands out of the way. He was an excellent dancer with a beautiful body, but smelled strongly of rum.

I was anxious to practice on this trip what I have learned in *reggaeton* class, but given the opportunity at this sultry party, I was too inhibited. I was afraid the locals would size me up as a white woman of a certain age looking foolish, dirty dancing with this young *cubano*. Also, our *salsera* friends do not approve of *reggaeton* and think it too vulgar. Anna, who loves our classes as much as I do, couldn't bring herself to let loose either. And I ask myself, why do we care so much about the good opinion of others? It is the scourge of womankind.

"Do you have a boyfriend? I mean a Cuban boyfriend," asked my dance partner.

"Well, yes ... but now, no."

"What happened?"

He laughed when I told him I had to give Paulo the boot and mimed kicking someone in the ass. He asked Anna if she had a Cuban boyfriend. Oh yes, she said. He grilled her: What is his name? How old is he? Where is he? How long have you known him? Finally she cracked, caught. He gave me a friendly, ear-piercing lecture. Never, he said, ever take on a Cuban boyfriend or husband. When you meet a man, tell him firmly that you are not interested in being his girlfriend or his wife. Choose your best candidate and take him as a lover, but no more—the first *cubano* to speak the truth about the Cuban love crisis.

"How old was your Cuban boyfriend?" he asked.

"Forty-four."

"Ay! An old man! Why bother with someone older than you? Take a young, strong man as your lover in Cuba!"

Amen, brother.

This morning I had an uninhibited dance-fest in the bathroom while getting ready. Loud, melodic Caribbean-Cuban music sailed up through the bathroom window. Marta informed me, with rolling eyes, that every Saturday morning, a party is held for the children, and the blaring music drives her crazy. I later stopped to observe the fiesta, and the woman at the door was happy to let me in, but the children were all sitting in their seats, not dancing as I'd expected. From the second floor vantage point, I noticed a small weekend flea market on the main street of Vedado. I went over and indulged my jewelry addiction by buying a few trinkets, and then walked the Malecón to the girls' place.

Catarina asked to join the walking tour I'd planned for Anna in Old Havana. Our first stop was the large market on the outskirts of the old town. The art is accessible, diverse, and beautiful in Cuba. I kick myself for not purchasing a street scene from one talented artist in particular. This country may soon change, never to be the same again.

We ended the tour at Taberna de la Muralla—where else? My singer invited me onstage once again, then came over at the end of the set and requested, with a most serious expression, to speak with me alone.

"I was the first man to ask you out when you arrived in Havana. I am jealous. And sad."

But he was not about to give up in the national pursuit; he carefully wrote out his email address and said the group was booked to play in Canada.

I nervously paced outside the apartment waiting for Anna and Catarina, who were late for our dinner reservation. I'd invited Javier to meet us at another street dance at the same location; I hate being late, even in a mañana culture. I'd called the small *paladar* last minute to get a table, and we were lucky to get one. They enticed us with a large lobster tail, and in spite of a 2001 travel book advising that lobsters have been put on the endangered species list in this region due to us greedy tourists, I guiltily followed Anna and Catarina's lead. A man, whom I assumed to be the owner, came to me with another set of menus.

"You have eaten here before, *si?*" he asked in Spanish.

Good memory.

"*Si.*"

He took our menus and gave us a new set with V.I.P. inscribed on the cover. Ah ha! So that is what the guidebook was referring to. I checked the prices, and they were lower than the ones on the original menu, the one I paid from on my first visit. *Paladares* have up to three menus with three different prices. If you have been in before, and they are feeling magnanimous, you may rate for a lower priced menu. The meal was delicious; the bill, a mess. It had Cornish game hens listed instead of lobster, and all the prices were wrong. It was only in the morning upon awakening that I remembered it is illegal for a *paladar* to sell lobster, hence the listed Cornish hens with a lesser price and the other items with the prices inflated. Imagine being forced to do business in such a way.

Catarina was as anxious as I to leave the restaurant for her rendezvous with Arturo. I easily spotted Javier wandering through the throng looking for me in his crisply pressed jeans, impeccable blue shirt, and academic shoes, looking conservative and out of place in the crowd. Karen sat entwined around Dauro, her new Cuban fixation. She was starry-eyed and had already fallen head over heels for him. Some are hard to spot, but I knew in a New York minute that this was one bad-assed boy. He was drinking low-grade rum from what looked like a child's juice box. He'd woven a fish tale to explain why he'd vanished the day before without a trace. Allegedly, he'd been stopped with a bag full of wooden statues carved by an artist friend on the way to the flea market. The police searched the bag, and because he did not have the appropriate license or identification, they took him to jail and confiscated the art. Now, he moaned to Karen, he would have to pay his friend the cost of the statues. Anna's earlier questions poked holes in his little fabrication. I watched the two of them together for a while and could not shut my mouth. I walked over to her.

"I realize you really don't know me, but I want you to promise me something."

"Okay."

"Promise me you will not give him one peso."

"I can promise you that. I don't have any extra to give, so I promise."

A shrunken middle-aged woman in a teen's ultra-mini skirt was working it with some suggestive dance moves, legs wide apart, butt in the air, occasionally gyrating on a man's lap. Anna danced with a spiked haired, collar-up-cool youth. I chuckled as she tore a strip off him for getting a little too friendly. God, she makes me laugh; when one of the men asked if he could have a drink of her water, her retort was, "Do you think I want your bacteria?"

Catarina had a glow as she danced with her man, the two smooth as silk together. As Javier and I leaned against a rail observing everyone, he told me he had called his mother that day to tell her about me.

Am I having *déjà vu*?

He watched the girls closely as they danced.

"The men dancing with your friends are only interested in getting money, you know."

"Oh, really?"

"Do you think when Cuban men tell stick-thin or unattractive foreign women that they are beautiful that they mean it? There are many beautiful women in Cuba. These men chase any foreign woman to take."

"And what makes me any different from my friends or other foreign women? I am certainly no more special."

"This is different, Wanda! You initiated a conversation with me. And I have never dated a foreign woman in Cuba. I honestly think you are an intelligent and pretty woman. This is much different than the situation with those *jineteros*."

I am beginning to feel like the dog in a Far Side cartoon that I once saw. The human is yammering away. All the dog hears is "Blah blah—Sparky— blah blah blah blah—Sparky—blah blah blah."

As though he were speaking about the weather, he said, "You know, my prick was very hard for you last night."

"Oh. You might not want to use that word."

"What—*prick?*" he articulated.

"Yes."

"No. I think it is fine."

On the walk to the taxis, Anna grilled Javier to test the validity of his credentials. I wasn't listening to the conversation, but afterwards she gave me a thumbs-up and left with the others in a taxi. Javier and I went to the corner bar for a nightcap. I figured I was on a roll. Why stop now?

"Where do you see this going?"

Pardon? I said nothing.

"What are you looking for in a man?"

I decided to play along with the game to see how far it would go, listing a long, impossible string of qualities. My mind wandered while he tried to convince me that he filled the requirements and then recited his needs in a woman. He told me he is a jealous man and that tonight he'd given a man who'd asked me to dance the signal to back off.

"Really?"

"*Si.*"

He demonstrated the Cuban signal, wagging his forefinger firmly back and forth (don't touch, she's mine).

"Hypothetically," he said, "If we were boyfriend-girlfriend, how often would you come to Cuba?"

I shrugged, thinking I might not return to Cuba for yet another twenty years.

"I would like if you came often, maybe every three months. Six months is too long."

Yes, yes, I thought, you too have heard of the money trees we foreigners have growing in our backyards.

"I have time to wait for you to be my girlfriend," he said.

Of course, what else is there *but* time on this prisoners' paradise island?

I sat and listened, saying nothing.

"You expose very little of yourself. I think you have a secret side you reveal to no one."

I grunted.

Next, he campaigned to spend New Year's Eve alone with me.

Sorry, not going to happen.

"Well, maybe you can convince your friends to have a small house party?"

Yes—I'm sure these *salseras* will want to spend New Year's Eve in the wild salsa capital of the world in a house. Without dance partners. Give your head a shake.

He walked me to the *casa* and we sat across the street on the cement fence.

"You are my Marilyn Monroe."

I am not completely immune to a comment like that from an attractive man, even if he is full of shit. He tried to persuade me to go into the lobby for privacy. My body had thawed from the hot salsa and sultry night air, but I said good night and went up to my room alone to fantasize about someone else.

Another late, late night.

New Year's Day

Sleepless in Havana. Yesterday, once again, I awoke far too early. Due to sleep deprivation, I have officially lost my ability to speak Spanish with any coherence. In spite of fatigue, I was in a good mood when I left for the long walk to the girls' *casita*.

When I arrived, Karen was engaged in an intense, teary-eyed discussion with Dauro on the tattered couch. I whizzed past to the kitchen. Nana immediately asked about "Shiny Shoes," the name she'd dubbed Javier with after noticing his gleaming footwear. They'd discussed him the night before and had given him the seal of approval.

"How did you find the cleanest cut guy in all of Havana?"

"Well, girls, he may be intelligent, well-educated and nicely put together, but he gets the boot too."

"Why?" they blurted in unison.

I gave them a synopsis of our relationship conversation, explaining that no matter his position, he too wanted out of this hellhole, and I looked like a prime candidate. His format was an eerie replica of Paulo's.

Karen wandered into the kitchen, shell-shocked. Anna asked for permission to share what had transpired and she acquiesced. She and Dauro had "broken up" because—surprise, surprise—he came over with a note he'd had painstakingly translated into English by a friend. The first ploy hadn't worked, so he came right out and asked for cash. She was heartbroken to discover that this was his objective all along, having thought they'd connected on a spiritual level. *A spiritual level?* Man, these guys are good. She was rather somber for the rest of the day.

The girls were anxious to get to a Santería street festival. Alvira, the *casa* owner, warned me not to keep my purse on my back, but to keep it in front of me at all times in this particular neighborhood.

As our entourage made its way, two neighborhood men began to follow. Anna politely told them to get lost; we did not want boyfriends. They convinced her they were good guys, neighbors after all, and only wanted to accompany us to the festival. We entered a small alleyway filled with people, strange art, and loud, festive music. I was immediately swept into a conversation with three men asking questions. I felt like a paranoid idiot, with my backpack protruding in front of me like a Buddha belly. They were inquisitive and personable. The rest of our group went inside the little building to look at the art. I was dehydrated and dizzy from the walk, but could only find a *cerveza* to quench my thirst, and it just added to my wooziness.

I later found the girls being lectured on Santería and Cuban culture by a well-dressed man of about fifty-five who was clearly proud of his expertise. Swarming around my friends was a group of men, one of whom I'd found to be sticky and clingy the first night we attended the street dance at the embassy.

After the lecture, Nana took a picture of our group. She carries a well-worn stuffed monkey in her purse on all her travels, and this monkey, Pongo, is in every photo. She'd placed him on my shoulder and stuck his arm in my silver hoop earring. Sticky

Guy jumped into the shot. Finding this little idiosyncrasy odd, I made a wisecrack about the traveling monkey. Sticky Guy made the assumption it was a derogatory remark about him. His face dropped as though he'd been slapped and he walked off dejectedly, no longer interested in us. I was horrified. I begged Anna to take the monkey in question to him and explain. She and Catarina tried, but there was no way. He wasn't buying it; he was convinced I'd called him a monkey. We were relieved to be rid of his group, but I had a stress stomachache afterwards as I worried about his hurt feelings.

The girls also had the original neighborhood twosome plus a third man buzzing around them. The trio asked to take us to a bar in Habana Vieja and everyone agreed to go, except Catarina who returned to the *casa* for a nap. We were in a decidedly bad neighborhood in Centro Habana, and the vibes were making Anna more anxious by the moment. Catarina had told us of her experience in the wee hours of the morning when returning with Arturo from his home. Only meters away, on the opposite side of the street, they'd come across a gang of teenage boys mugging two tourists, one of whom was very drunk. The drunk one was being kicked and beaten. This would not be a pleasant sight on a holiday or any time.

To punctuate Anna's mood, she stepped in dog poop and somehow it got smeared on the side of her leg. One of the men tried to help, but only made it worse. We bought our water supply for the long walk and got to the Malecón, *tout de suite*. The Cubans asked us to follow them a distance behind, so as not to alert the police, and that suited us fine. We walked endlessly in the heat and finally came to what I recognized as the end of the Old Havana zone. The dingy street they waved us down was less than inviting, and we all agreed we'd had enough. Anna skillfully got rid of the men by giving them a small amount of money to buy drinks for their efforts. It satisfied them and they went on their way.

I have come to the conclusion that my September trip, by mere chance, was the fantasyland version of Havana, due to *La Cumbre*. The combination of the lack of tourists and the enormous number of police everywhere kept the hustlers at home, and I was able to enjoy the good people of Havana. I am grateful for having had that Cuban moment.

I took a fitful siesta before the New Year's Eve festivities began and then joined the girls at the *casa*. I was to call Javier with the details, but decided to stand him up. It is not my style when I have made plans with someone. I have been raised to be nice—Saskatchewan nice—and if you've ever visited a farm in Saskatchewan, you'll know what kind of nice I'm talking about. But niceness has gotten me into jams before. (Do you remember how I ended up with the Stalker Fax Repairman because I thought I should be nice?) It almost killed me to refrain from calling to cancel, but I knew if I did, it would mean having a long-winded and pointless debate.

Dressed in her best, Marta buzzed around the apartment in preparation for New Year's Eve, and asked for my approval of her outfit. She handed me a small box with a filigree pendant inside, kissed me on the cheek, and wished me a Happy New Year. She raced out the door excitedly to meet her dinner date. Her boys had gone to spend the evening with their father. The apartment was dark and unusually silent.

When I arrived at the girls' *casa*, I gratefully accepted Alvira's invitation to eat the ample leftovers. Dinner was a simple but delicious stew of garbanzo beans and beef. Arturo and I chatted while the girls got ready. I found him to be a soft-spoken and intelligent man. He has a degree in mechanical engineering, but is out of work. He told me he was concerned about the location of this *casa*; it was located in a particularly dangerous neighborhood, and he felt it was an unsafe place for the girls to stay. That was my gut feeling about the area when I first saw it, but I thought I was overreacting. If a *habanero* thought it was dangerous, I wasn't off the mark. When I left Anna later that night, I made her promise that none of them would walk home alone again, as Karen had done the night before. She also promised me that the girls would insist that the taxis take them to the door, rather than dropping them a few blocks away on the Prado, as was the custom.

I'd left the New Year's Eve planning to the group, since I was crashing their vacation and didn't want to insinuate myself into their agenda with demands. Maybe I should have put in my two cents' worth. They'd debated too long and most events were sold out. We walked to the Hotel Deauville to find a taxi, and there we met a friend of Arturo's, a gorgeous, make-your-panties-drop *cubano*. In my books, there's nothing like a handsome, dark-skinned man in a good white shirt and hot jeans. Before we all jumped into the antiquated, '50s American taxi (illegal for tourists), which Cubans call *almendróns*, I told Beautiful he was just that.

"Pretty bold, aren't we?" asked Nana.

"Couldn't resist."

Our *almendrón* was outfitted with a good sound system, with *reggaeton* blasting. Our driver was obviously a man about town.

Salón Rojo, around the corner from my *casa*, was lined up down the block; I could have easily gotten us tickets that morning. A pow-wow ensued. I was silently disappointed that we had not made reservations someplace exciting, so that I could do something grand to redeem the trip.

We bombed over to a utilitarian looking building with two clubs and paid our taxi driver ten times the rate he'd have gotten with a Cuban fare, but it was well worth it for the entertainment we'd gotten in the cab. I lost my equanimity when I was told it was mandatory that I leave my purse at the coat check inside the club. At this point in the trip, it was like handing the booty over to the pirates.

In the club, I had another Overstuffed and Dullard sighting, but this time Overstuffed had a *cubana* in tow. He looked just as bored and as boring as ever, and I felt overwhelming sympathy for the poor young girl who had to prostitute herself to this unappealing man.

The club was small, sparsely filled, and sorely lacking in any hint of festivity, but we were at the beggars-can't-be-choosers stage. A young *cubano*, who sat with two Spanish women and an older black man, asked me to dance.

"*¡Más suave!*" (more gently), he instructed me as he danced off the beat.

Más suave, my ass. I sat down abruptly.

Nana sat in misery, disappointed by the *reggaeton* music and lack of men to dance with, even if the salsa band should ever begin. She is the only one who's not been besieged by the men so far and I am curious; they seem to have no criteria. They pursue all types, all sizes, and all ages of women. The only thing I can fathom is that she is strong and masculine looking, and maybe that is where the macho Cuban draws the line.

I found it apropos that on December 31st—the eve of the Anniversary of the Triumph of the Revolution—directly in front of us was a huge, brightly lit mural of Che Guevara. It mesmerized me for a portion of the evening, and the thought lurked in the back of my mind that if another *revolución* were to occur, in light of Castro's infirmity, the anniversary date might be an excellent choice. The tensions are running so high that the backstreets of Havana feel like a pressure cooker ready to blow. I am sure that the couples and families in the heart of the tourist zone or in the Disneyland atmosphere of Varadero do not feel these vibes, but as a single woman exploring the core of Havana and fraternizing in the streets with the inhabitants of this city, I feel the intense sense of frustration, anger and desperation. And desperation can make people do very bad things.

A group of Arturo's friends came in, and he urged them to ask Nana and Karen to dance. Someone introduced me to a professional basketball player who held no attraction for me. Catarina came to tell us that Beautiful from the hotel was on the phone and he would like to join us; however, we would have to pay his way. Nobody was willing, and that included me. The allure is lost with this unwavering prerequisite. It is like having a bucket of ice water thrown on a blazing fire. Pssssssssssssst— there goes the lust, up in smoke.

The band began at one-bloody-thirty in the morning; that's pushing it, even in a Latin country. The all-girl group were pretty to look at, but not overly talented. Anna walked me out to find a taxi and a young man in a dilapidated, barely running, unofficial Lada "taxi" waited in front of the registered taxi line-up. He asked a ridiculous fare, and I turned to grab a legitimate taxi in a decent car at this hour in God Knows Where, Havana. But Anna insisted on negotiating with the driver, and he agreed to a normal fare.

As soon as we drove off, he raised one eyebrow and commented on my perfume, and we headed off into a wooded area near the club. As we meandered through this backwoods, I saw my life flash before my eyes. *Is this it?* I thought. I knew we were next to the Plaza de la Revolución, but I'd lost my bearings. *Now where in the hell am I and why did I get into this beat up, illegal taxi?* I made it to the last night of this bizarre vacation without physical harm. Is my number up?

When we exited the wooded area and onto a busy street, I heaved a sigh. The driver's slang Spanish was the worst I'd yet heard, almost incomprehensible. I'm sure he took me the long way home just for entertainment, but I didn't care, as long as I made it to the door of the *casita*.

As we pulled up, I spotted Kaarlo, a Finnish man staying at Marta's whom I'd met in passing earlier, entering the gate of the building. He was an attractive, energetic man of close to fifty. He asked me to leave the gate ajar for his sweetheart, and invited me to sit on the patio for a nightcap of Baileys and wine. The thin black girl who I'd seen yesterday morning came in, and Kaarlo introduced us and poured drinks. He informed us that he was starving and had to go get a pizza down the street before settling in for a drink; then he left us on our own. The girl had two scars on the side of her lovely face and she kept playing with her long ponytail. She was dressed in low-rise jeans, and a tiny halter top, a glittery belt, and large hoop earrings. She spoke no English and she had a slight lisp, so with her Havana Spanish, I found it a challenge to converse with her. She was warm and friendly and told me she and Kaarlo had been seeing each other for three and a half years. Who knew what time it was by then, so I went to bed. I was too weary to wait for Kaarlo, even though I wanted to learn more about their situation. Inquiring minds want to know.

In the morning, everyone was buzzing around the house. Marta was busy cooking, chatting with Alessandro the Italian, whom I'd seen only in passing. The other Italian, a chain-smoking women situated in the tiny room off of the kitchen, breezed by with her cigarette in hand. *"Buon giorno, buon giorno!"*

Kaarlo walked by excitedly and put a new CD in the stereo to share with us. His girlfriend slowly stretched her arms and legs while walking through the living room, clearly comfortable in her surroundings. I sat with Alessandro over breakfast and we attempted a conversation in *Italish*. He is from Venice and on the door, he'd posted a colorful calendar of his mystical home city. The *casa* was far too interesting to leave for a planned walk to see the girls before my departure.

Kaarlo pulled me into the living room to listen to his new CD, which was fantastic, and told me that the Cuban group playing had defected to France. He is a steward for a Finnish airline and vented about the Americans he'd dealt with on his flights. He confirmed that he and Bella had met three and a half years ago and that he visits Cuba five or six times a year and stays with Marta each time. He explained that he'd had many Finnish girlfriends, but they all wanted marriage and it wasn't for him, so he enjoyed the arrangement he had here in Cuba with Bella. He makes sure she is taken care of financially. She has a child (I didn't ask if it was his) and if she needs anything, she comes to Marta and he refunds her when he returns. He'd visited her family for the first time last night before they'd gone to Salón Rojo (for a real Havana New Year's Eve party) and said he was now glad he'd been helping her out financially, after seeing the abject poverty she'd come from. He has traveled the world extensively and been in shady places, but he found the neighborhood extremely intimidating, despite his large stature and heavily muscled body.

 I returned to the kitchen and begged for another delicious *café con leche*. Marta informed me that Bella didn't eat enough and was too skinny and tried to hide it by layering her underpants. She then pulled Bella in the kitchen to confirm this by showing me the layers of panties she was wearing to conceal her thinness and fill out her jeans. Bella was mute as Marta lovingly berated her and pulled at her clothing. I was unsure of what to say to that.

 The Italian woman walked by again, leaving a trail of smoke. She mumbled something to me that I did not understand in the least, but I smiled back anyway.

 After packing, I went down to the main street of Vedado to buy my baristas back at home some Cuban cigarettes and cigars. You know I make tobacco purchases with great reluctance. I also bought Añejos rum from a market off the beaten path. There was a pretty boxed set of espresso cups in the little gift area, so I waited to purchase one for Marta. In the line, a woman behind me sniffed at me the whole way. I suppose expensive perfume is not common here.

 I stopped to give a Canada cap to the guard down the street who'd been flirting with me since I arrived. He beamed in front of his friends and insisted on getting my email address, telling me to expect a letter shortly. I could not embarrass him, so gave him my address, knowing we would have nothing to communicate about.

Marta came to my door to announce the taxi and help me with my bags. My earth angel had a wonderful lunch packed, and my bill was far less than I'd anticipated, with no charge for her efficient laundry service (she'd caught me washing out some of my things and insisted on washing all of my laundry). She sent me off with a profusion of kisses and hugs, making me promise to write her soon, painting the world with her endless sweetness.

"Many people in Cuba will be sad that you are leaving," she said in Spanish.

She knew Rene, my driver, and he asked if his wife could join us on the trip to Varadero. They were a lovely couple, obviously in love. They'd known each other for thirty years and had parted when they were young and married other people. They reconnected and discovered both were divorced, and now they'd been married for five years. We kept each other entertained and I told them the stories of the past two weeks, but I couldn't have conjugated a Spanish verb if my life depended on it. I gave them a Reader's Digest version of the Paulo story. They laughed loudly when I told them that had I been looking for a *jinetero*, I would have chosen a younger one with a much better body.

I arrived to a house crammed with Ricardo's relatives when I went to pick up my suitcase at the scene of the crime. Malita was warm and not in the least upset that I had changed my plans and cancelled my last two days at their *casa*. I told her about my Paulo and girlfriend sighting on Obispo and she shook her head in disgust. I would have enjoyed being able to communicate better with her; I think she is a good woman.

At the airport, Rene and his wife bade me the warm farewell of family. A line-up of a thousand tourists greeted me. What was I thinking, traveling on New Year's Day?

As I was on my way to pay the tourist fee, a woman whizzed by rapidly repeating, "*Si, mi amor. Si, mi amor.*"

I looked over and saw that the woman was none other than Maria, another acquaintance who had recently married a Cuban. She quickly introduced her sizeable husband and ran off to catch her plane.

I went outside to a small kiosk to get my very last Bucanero beer. I was glad to spend the time outside looking at the blue sky, rather than in the cloying, smoky bar upstairs. I saw Maria's husband wandering around, and later, he and another Cuban left with a freshly landed foreign woman. I wondered whether she was with him or his friend.

¿Quién sabe?

Nine
Back to the Future

© Wanda St.Hilaire

Of course, out of every hundred adventures you embark on, ninety-nine don't work out the way you hoped. I've been blanket-tossed and I've been bruised; still, nothing can compare with waiting for the next adventure.
–Miguel (de) Cervantes
Spanish Novelist, Playwright and Poet

I sit on the plane and I am too fatigued and brain-fogged to open my laptop or read a book. I let the faces and events of Cuba pass through my mind like movie clips in bits and bites. I think of women I know and other women I don't know who have innocently entangled themselves with the men of the beautiful island I have just left. I understand all too well; I am flying back into a business-class culture that does not feed a woman's soul or anyone's sensuality. We go through the motions of our lives, too busy to identify what is missing, only knowing that we have a small yet painful ache in our hearts or our bodies or both. I recall the poem I wrote after returning home to the carnal void from my first long-term winter sojourn on the steamy coast of Mexico:

> *Icemen*
>
> *cold, insinuating stares*
> *they starve us of tender smiles*
> *of playful lust*
> *leaning, sipping with cool façades*
>
> *they wait and watch*
> *selecting their prey for night's end*
>
> *I live in a land of extinct passion*
> *a lost art*
> *how did they get here*
> *all these Icemen?*

One day, we take a trip, maybe to Cuba, maybe to Capri, and we come alive in ways we did not know we could. We become the women we have always wanted to be, always known we were: beautiful, sensuous, glowing, and vibrating with sexual energy. Like wilted flowers living in cracks of cement, we are transplanted into a lush tropical jungle and watered with the attentions of hot-blooded men who think we are beautiful, even if we don't fit the image of a magazine. We are seduced and intoxicated, awash in a cascade of pheromones as powerful and persuasive as any opiate. Like travelers in a dry desert, we do not believe we are seeing only a mirage; we believe we have arrived at the oasis. Only when we endeavor to bring the oasis home do we realize it was only a mirage and cannot sustain itself. Then, it evaporates before our eyes. We think we can transplant hot, tropically grown men and that the cold, harsh environment we plant them into will not reject them. But what is the true success rate of these transplants?

The radical variances between a Cuban life and a Canadian life pass through my mind. Glaringly, there is the utter contrast in culture and language. Cubans are a people who live on the street, in the heat and the pulse of music that runs through their veins, imprinted in each cell of their bodies. What is music to us? We do not have songs handed down from generation to generation that move us to the core, inciting passion and patriotism—songs that make us dance in the street in harmony and understanding, bonding us to each other. (God forbid we should dance in the street at all). The salsa and African rhythms are thematic every day, all day, wherever you go in Cuba. *Son* defines the music that moves the bodies of the Cubans sensually and beautifully in ways we can only hope to imitate, but will never be able to replicate authentically.

Cubans walk and interact with each other every single day and feel the ground beneath their feet and the humidity on their skin. We climb into the mechanically controlled weather systems of our vehicles each day, detached from the grounding of our bodies to the earth. We drive long distances to see each other and to get to our endlessly varying destinations. What must they think of our harsh winters when they arrive to find us scraping ice and snow off our cars, living under layers of heavy clothing, boots and scarves, and freezing up the minute we step outside?

We whiz past each other, unconnected from our neighbors, individually encapsulated in our own lives and unconcerned about the condition of the lives of others. Cubans live in commune style, crammed together in close quarters. One does not feel anonymous in Cuba, even as a foreigner. Although we in our culture share a country, we each live a completely different reality because of our freedom of choice. How do Cubans feel when separated from their street life and the commonality of living side by side under a regime that has dictated their condition throughout their lives? (The émigrés are inevitably under the age of forty-eight).

We have freedom of speech and can draw cartoons, sing songs, or protest in front of Parliament about any subject we choose. We can bash our politicians and the system in the streets, in cafes, in our homes, in the press, and on TV, without consequence. We can travel anywhere at any time, both because we are allowed to and because we can afford to do so.

We take our endless cornucopia of food for granted. Food is another nucleus of Cuban culture. Although we view their diet as bland and limited, it is the centre of life in Cuba and another commonality and comfort that we can't possibly comprehend. I imagine the diversity of meals I would find if I were to, on any given night, visit each home in Calgary, alone: barbequed steaks, roasted chickens, hamburgers, fish, seafood, pork, turkey, eggs, fast food, frozen food, vegetarian meals, pizza, crackers with cheese and fruit, sandwiches, soups in every flavor, an endless array of vegetables, some meals with rice, some potatoes, some pasta, some bread, and then the ethnic food; Indian, Chinese, Italian, Japanese, Salvadoran, Croatian, Ukrainian, German....

Then I imagine if I were to visit each home in *all* of Cuba on that same night. In all likelihood I would find rice, beans, and a little pork in a vast majority of homes. This is a reassuring certainty for Cubans. When they come to Canada, it must leave a hole in their daily existence not to have that certainty. I am sure their senses are assaulted by the strange and unfamiliar food they are presented with: the sweet, spicy, pungent, aromatic, grainy, savory, bitter, and battered, as well as the profusion of oils, vinegars, sauces, herbs, and condiments, to say nothing of the multitude of ethnic restaurants we frequent. When Cubans enter a grocery store for the first time in Canada, are they overwhelmed with the abundance, the heaps of vegetables and fruit, the selections of meats, the mountains of bread, the rows of foods that they have never seen before?

I think of Santería and how this mysterious religion influences the islanders. I wonder how many Cubans go to their *babalaos* for advice and help with the problems of their lives, or at least live by some of Santería's values and beliefs. With our pragmatic lives, we can view this religion as silly and superstitious. We once many years ago had our own *babalaos*, but we called them witches and burned them at the stake, and that was the end of that. The *babalaos* are mystical and magical "sorcerers"; they are revered and are a part of everyday life, even for no-nonsense Cuban engineers.

When we bring a man or a woman home from Cuba, we may not consider that we are, in essence, time traveling that person fifty years into the future. Although they see the North American culture on illegal TV, and by observing tourists and communicating with their Miami relatives, they are not living it. They can imagine it but are not steeped in the fast pace of Western culture.

Their dilapidated American cars from the '50s are still functioning, as if by miracle, and their rusty Russian Ladas are running on a wing and a prayer. They cannot drive down to the car dealer of their choice, call up their bank, and pick out a new shiny vehicle on a whim. Their economy works through simple exchanges of cash for goods. They do not live with debit cards, credit cards, frequent user cards, air miles, discount cards, multitudes of bank accounts, investments, and debt. They do not make a hobby of shopping in massive malls with access to a barrage of brand labels and miles of commercialism and capitalist materialism. They live with outmoded computers and phone systems discarded long ago by other countries. Their Internet access is extremely limited, slow, and antiquated. There are no fake tits, step-aerobic bodies, lyposuctioned thighs, botoxed brows, and faces that have been surgically lifted; what Mother Nature provides is what a Cuban gets. The Cubans' one luxury is the simplicity of life on the island.

How well would I adapt and assimilate if I were sent to live fifty years into the future in a different country, with a new language and culture *and* a new foreign husband? Nothing is impossible, and every person adapts in his or her own way; however, it seems to me that the odds are stacked high against a cross-cultural Cuban marriage while the transitions and acclimatization occurs. Also, it would be reasonable to question the sincerity behind a Cuban's pursuit of a foreigner.

I have taken for granted my good fortune once again and I am reminded of how rich we are and how blessed and free I am. I say my simple prayer. *Thank you.*

Some may admire Castro for his long stranglehold on his country, for his alliances, for keeping the Americans out and outwitting the CIA at the Bay of Pigs, *and* surviving 638 alleged assassination attempts. Yes, he has done all of this, but at what price? Many visitors argue that the people are happy with their condition. I have only scratched the surface of all that Cuba is, but as I sit on this plane, I feel a profound sadness for the people of Cuba, for the loss of their innocence and their gradual transformation, as pride erodes into desperation.

Adiós, La Habana.

January 8th, 2007
A New Year

I begin the New Year with a slow start, back from Cuba, feeling tired and foggy. I have not felt like working, and my apartment is in a state of disorganization because of scattered paperwork.

Upon returning, I awoke to a dream of a girl being thrown into my beach house through a window. She was covered in sand and wearing a pretty dress. She had been with a well-known Cuban, and he had tried to drown her and then hide her. She was alive, but dazed and disoriented.

Darshana remained well-hidden, probably on purpose, at the sardine-packed airport in Cuba, in spite of the fact that we were on the same flight. We saw each other only when we reached the baggage area in Canada. Apparently, she'd booked the bus transfer to Havana from the tour rep as I'd recommended, but the bus had left without her.

The baristas were thrilled with their foreign cigarettes and cigars. I found that my café had been outfitted in comfy couches and chairs. The décor is great for my writing, and keeps me there for even longer sessions. A couple sat down nearby speaking Spanish, and I couldn't help turning to eavesdrop. I apologized when they noticed, saying I'd just returned from Cuba and that I was irresistibly drawn to the language. Irony was at play; they are from my beloved second home. He is a writer and was a professor of literature in Mexico City. I wore my Guevara pendant, and the Che postcards fell out of my journal as he wrote down some suggested reading. They revealed that he is writing a book—the key character: Che Guevara. He has been to Argentina to interview Che's nanny and friends. We were abuzz, and I insisted that he email me when the book was completed.

On my second day back, I awoke to another bad dream about Cuba. Javier also emailed. He sent a simple note, with a big kiss, and a file with three photos of himself attached. There was no mention of the fact that I had stood him up on New Year's Eve. He asked me to send him some pictures of myself. For a *momentito*,

I was tempted to play, but I slapped myself and wrote him that it was pointless, since I have no intention of returning to Cuba.

I wrote a scathing email to Paulo when I returned home. It was not my high point in emotional maturity. I will admit that I took great pleasure in warning him to watch his back on the streets of Havana. I informed him that I'd been to both the Canadian Consulate and the police with his picture, and that they were none too happy with the story, and were looking for him. I'd done nothing of the sort, but hoped the letter would succeed in keeping him away from vulnerable foreign women. At home, such a threat would be scoffed at, but in Cuba, it is an everyday possibility that one will be thrown in jail for mere suspicion of any small misdemeanor. I also wanted him to feel as nervous as I had on the streets of Old Havana, at least for a while. I had the satisfaction of knowing he'd received the email when I received his jumbled, one-line insult in return.

I visited Malik at his new restaurant to ask if his cousins had told him that they'd met me on the beach in Varadero.

"Did you tell them we did not have sex?" he asked desperately.

"Now, why would I tell them that?"

He asked me to state for the record that we never had sex, but in the same breath, he wondered if I would have an affair with him. I know he is only kibitzing. His religious beliefs would not allow him to have sex with me when he was single, so I am sure he could not do it now that he has a wife and children. He called his cousin Jamal while I was there and left a message that I was in the café, mentioned our meeting, and said that we had not had sex when we were dating. What a nut.

He sat down and told me a story about a relative who was living in Cuba. One family had emigrated to Cuba from Lebanon in the early 1900s. His uncle went to Cuba and found a cousin living in abject poverty in a little house made of wooden two-by-fours. He was using a pop can as a glass, and had only one fry pan.

The uncle returned to Canada and asked each family to donate $200 for his next trip to give to this *pobresito*. He raised $4000 and went back to visit the cousin. His plan was to give him the money and discuss what to do with it. Should he open a bank account? What did he want to buy and how much did he want to save? The uncle handed the man the cash and in a frenzy of excitement, the man ran off with it in hand like a mad hyena. He's never been seen or heard from again, and they are disappointed because they want to give him more. Allah only knows what happened to him.

I finally unpacked, keeping the television on for company. A program called *Very Bad Men* caught my attention. It featured a true story about a slick, handsome Frenchman who'd gone to Los Angeles and conned a pretty blond woman, as well as a slew of shrewd businessmen. This fellow was extremely smooth in his plot, so bore no resemblance to Paulo, but still, this was another irony.

Gabriel, the Spaniard, called once again on the weekend. He wanted to know how my trip went and we discussed the desperate situation of the people of Cuba. I told him of a friend who'd been taken twice by beautiful women in Cuba for a significant amount of cash. My friend is a savvy world traveler and is a university professor—not a stupid man, yet he is still susceptible to the wiles of the clever *jinetera*.

Werner, the Austrian, has also written. His email was crisp and pleasant and he said I am welcome to visit Hamburg anytime. He said he'd gotten a parasite as a parting present from his last meal out with me at La Dominica. But who, I ask, eats carpaccio in Cuba?

On Saturday night, I found a long-stemmed red rose on my doorstep from my neighbor Jane. Later, there was a knock at my door. On the doorstep lay a piece of exquisite (still warm) French chocolate cake wrapped in a red ribbon that had been left by my neighbor Karen. I am forever grateful for the sisterhood of the women who surround me.

Epilogue

If you're looking for monogamy,
you'd better marry a swan.
—Nora Ephron
US Writer
(*Heartburn*)

One Year Later

Lola never laid eyes on her father. He deemed it too risky to meet the fruit of his own loins. Her mother, Carrie, has since met a young, sexy Bolivian and visited him recently in South America.

Gaby, whose Cuban husband arrived in Canada in September, asked him to leave in January. In February, while playing what looked a lot like piggies in a blanket with one of her dance acquaintances, her husband called to ask for a monthly stipend for his new life in Canada.

Remember Maria's oversized husband who'd left the airport with a different foreign woman? He never made it to Canada; Maria ended the relationship before the immigration papers were even processed. The relationship ended as quickly as it began.

Three and a half years into the marriage, Ashley's husband has still not arrived in Canada, due to some extraordinary governmental red-tape delays. She frequently commutes to Cuba.

Catarina wisely left the happy memory of Arturo behind and has since fallen in love at home with a wonderful Québécois.

Cassandra, the artist who was married to the television addict, has since left her marriage.

Gabriel, the Spaniard, still calls looking for the Canadian with the Andalucían smile, offering his second home by the sea if I visit Spain.

Alejandro emailed eleven months after my return from Cuba. He wanted to meet up on the coast of Mexico.

A few months after returning from Cuba, I ended the dance with Miguel. His heart was encased in a ring of ice too fortified to allow him to give anything of himself other than his body. As I pray for Cuba's emancipation, I also pray for his.

Paulo has never been heard from nor seen again. He could be sitting in a Cuban prison somewhere for subversive activity. He could be on Cuba's Most Wanted list. Who knows?

As for me, I finally made it to Oaxaca, Mexico, firstly in September for a magical two-week vacation. Smitten with the place, I returned for a one-month writing sojourn over Christmas.

Before I left, my editor asked me to journal about a seemingly easy yet poignant question: *why are you writing this book?* It would be a simple enough task, I thought. My knee-jerk answer morphed as I journalized each day in the poinsettia-filled square over my morning latte.

Amidst the events of my trip, an experience in Oaxaca brought an epiphany. A fascinating Mexican man I'd met on my first trip had taken me out for my birthday. The next morning, I sat drying my hair in the living room of my apartment, admiring the flowers around me.

Then I *really* looked at the flowers. The bouquet I'd bought myself, a gorgeous selection of the largest, most fragrant white lilies I'd ever seen, spoke to me. I listened. The massive spray of white calla lilies also sang out from the bedroom, knowing they had my attention. They conveyed volumes. I looked over at the simple bouquet of alstroemerias my date had given me, and then I looked back at the lilies. My eyes darted back and forth between the bouquets.

I love all flowers and had been happy to receive them; I'd not been given flowers from a man for many years. Yet something had nagged at me the night before when I said good night to my Mexican date at the door of my *casita*. And it now bothered me.

Awareness exploded in me. This man was not a simple *campesino*; he was a highly acclaimed, financially successful artist. I'd been to his impressive studio-gallery and saw that he had an eye for beauty. His work was full of sensuality, color, and vibrancy. He intimately knew the difference between the beautiful and the ordinary. In my moment of awareness, I knew that he'd thought the token bouquet would get me into his bed. He didn't need to make a grand gesture with an exquisite arrangement, in spite of his reticence since my departure in September. Further still, I came to the painful realization that it was I who'd set the stage, I who'd demonstrated that I'd accept so little.

The lilies whispered, "You accept far less than you deserve. And when you settle for less than you deserve, you receive an even further diminished version of what you accept."

Crumbs, I thought. All my life I have accepted the crumbs from the hearts of men. They were fun, they were memorable, they were exciting and some were generous of pocket, but I'd attracted the commitment-phobes, and a couple of *bandidos*—men who were not prepared to give from the deepest part of their heart or with generosity of spirit. It did not escape me that these men served as a mirror to my own bruised and guarded heart, a heart in dire need of restoration and repair.

This man was a perfect example of an imposter, a fake loaf. You've tasted the type of bread that, when you bite into it, collapses and sticks to the roof of your mouth. It is without substance or nutrition. This man seduced me with his sophistication, intelligence, and creative success. I'd believed he was a whole-loaf kind of man and got swept, as though caught in an undertow, into the exotic excitement that he offered. But as I reviewed my experience with him, I saw that he was yet another crumb-giver wearing the clever guise of a full loaf.

I examined my past with men with crystal clarity and I saw a long trail of tiny crumbs leading to this day of revelation. They had made small gestures that I'd fooled myself into believing were sustenance. I'd pushed aside my deep longing for love for a long time. For the sake of adventure, I'd forsaken myself.

I sensed an irrevocable shift in that moment. In the recesses of my subconscious, this knowledge had always been present; it had been tugging at my conscious mind for many a year. I'd dreamt of a pretty little girl dressed in a white pinafore in a secret, untamed garden, patiently waiting for me on a bench behind the high walls of the garden. She'd even visited me in a vivid meditation. In it, she leapt up to greet me and took my hand to show me all the magic that lay hidden in the garden. There was no trace of malice in her demeanor, no recriminations—nothing but joy. She ran and twirled and did somersaults in delight at my arrival. I was asked to accept her, to embrace her. As I did, a bolt ripped through my heart, my chest heaved and I let forth a sob. I saw her beauty and joie de vivre. I cried for how much I missed her. How could I abandon such a lovely, vibrant child? Still, she looked at me with only unconditional love. Although deeply moved at the time, I had forgotten, become caught up in the amnesia-inducing web of "real" life, and once again left her to languish alone behind the walls of the garden.

Even with the *fula* that Paulo was, I had not yet been prepared to admit to myself this lifelong pattern. But now, as the reasons that I'd accepted so little and the justifications for doing so lined up in my mind, they fell just as quickly. Once revealed, the inextricable pull, the attachments, and the illusions dissolved.

Finally, it was the flowers I've loved since my first spring crocus as that little girl that liberated me. At the moment I really looked at those flowers in Oaxaca with new eyes, I understood perfectly why I was writing this book.

Acknowledgements

Firstly, I would like to thank my editor, Rona Altrows, for your patience with my endless questions. I have gained a new appreciation for every novel and memoir ever birthed into reality. Also, thank you to Ryan Fitzgerald, my techie and proofreader extraordinaire.

Thank you to my family and friends for your encouragement and enthusiasm. Nino and Eduardo of Latin Corner Dance Studio—thank you for brightening up my life with your *dominicano* joie de vivre.

To my aunties Kay and Donna … finally! The first of my travel memoirs is out in the world—I hope not too scandalous for the family coffer.

And *muchisima gracias* to you, the reader, for accompanying me on my journey.

Glossary

abuela - grandmother
abuelita - diminutive form of grandmother
adiós - good-bye
almendróns - literally, big almonds
amiga/amigo - friend
amore (Italian) - love
babalao - Santerían priest
bandido - outlaw, bandit, desperado
baños - bathrooms
Bonjour! Ça va? (French) - Hello; good morning! How are you?
buenas noches - good night
buon giorno (Italian) - good morning
Ça va bien, merci, et vous? (French) - I am well, thank you, and you?
café con leche - strong espresso-like coffee with hot milk
caliente - hot (horny)
calle - street
campesino - peasant/countryman/farmer
casa/casita - house/little house
casas particulares - bed and breakfast style accommodations
cerveza - beer
chica - girl
cojónes - balls
congri - red beans and rice

cubana/o - Cuban woman/man
dulce - sweet
Durmiendo con el Enemigo - Sleeping with the Enemy
el banco - the bank
en español - in Spanish
España - Spain
faire l'amour - lovemaking
fattoush - Arabic salad
filloas - large crepes
fula - fucked up person or situation
gracias - thank you
Habana Vieja - Old Havana
habanero/a - a resident of Havana
hasta pronto - until soon, see you soon
hola - hello/hi
jalapeño - small green hot pepper
je ne comprend pas (French) - I don't understand
jinetero - male hustler/man who dates/sleeps with foreigners for financial gain (literally means jockey)
jinetera - female hustler/woman who dates/sleeps with for foreigners for financial gain
La Cumbre - The Convention (Summit Convention)
la dulce vida - the sweet life
La Guajira - literally - a woman from the countryside (bumpkin)
lluvia de oro - gold rain
ma chère - my dear
mais, c'est la vie - but, such is life
malanga - a root vegetable resembling a sweet potato
Malecón - seafront boardwalk, pier
mañana - tomorrow
más suave - more smoothly, gentle

menstruación - menstruation
merde (French) - shit
mi - my
mi princesa - my princess
mojito - a delicious drink of rum, soda water, sugar, lime juice, and fresh mint leaves
moles - rich Mexican traditional sauces
momentito - a very brief moment
mon amie (French) - my friend (female)
mon Dieu (French) - my God
moneda nacional - Cuban peso (MN)
moros y cristianos - Moors and Christians (black beans and rice)
moviendo la cintura - moving the waist/hips
muralla - wall
muy - very
nacional - national
non (French) - no
novela - soap opera
novia - girlfriend
oeuf (French) - egg
paladar - privately owned restaurant
palapa – palm-leafed umbrella or roof
panzón - fat-bellied man
Patria o Muerte - Homeland or Death
pastelería - dessert/pastry shop
Período Especial - Special Period
picante - hot, spicy
pobresito - poor man (poor thing)
por favor - please
¿porque? - why
princesa - princess

qué lástima - too bad, what a pity
qué linda - how pretty
¿Quién es? - Who is it?
¿Quién sabe? - Who knows?
quinceañera - a rite of passage into womanhood in some Latin cultures that is celebrated on a girl's fifteenth birthday
reggaeton - dirty dancing Latin style ("doggy-style")
revolución - revolution
salseras - serious (female) salsa dancers
sans (French) - without
señor - mister, sir, gentleman
si - yes
si, mi amor - yes, my love
Son - With roots on the island of Cuba, *Son Cubano* is a style of music that became popular in the second half of the 19th century in the eastern province of Oriente. The earliest known son dates from the late 1500s (the oldest known son is "Son de la Má Teodora," from about the 1570s in Santiago de Cuba). It combines the structure and elements of Spanish canción and the Spanish guitar with African rhythms and percussion instruments of Bantu and Arara origin. (from Wikipedia - The Free Encyclopedia)
taberna - tavern/bar
tagine - Arabic stew
tamal - a steamed cornhusk stuffed with cornmeal (masa) and various meats
tienda - shop or store
tout de suite (French) - quickly, right away
tranquila - be calm
ven - come
ven aquí - come here
vino - wine

Wanda's Wicked Words

flubbery - wiggly, loose, cellulite-laden skin
hork - to cough up phlegm in a loud, extremely disgusting manner
Italish - a combination of Italian and Spanish
pervy - perverted personality
Spidey senses - from *Spider-Man*: tingly, intuitive sensation
toad-esque - looking like a large toad
twitterpated - a euphoric state of butterflies and sexual excitement. (Used frequently by my friend Lynne. It is from the movie *Bambi*.)

If you have not seen the old movie *Shirley Valentine*, I highly recommend it!

Suggested reading: *The End of America* by Naomi Wolf.

Discover other titles by Wanda St.Hilaire:

Of Love … Life … and Journeys
ISBN # 1-894331-10-9

A New Life - A New Baby Boy
ISBN # 1-894331-00-1

A New Life - A New Baby Girl
ISBN # 1-894331-01-X

Graduate - A Little Roadmap to Your Dreams
ISBN # 1-894331-02-8

My Love…
ISBN # 1-894331-03-6

To You My Friend
ISBN # 1-894331-05-2

For Your Marriage I Wish…
ISBN # 1-894331-04-4

Newly Single Woman - A Celebration of Freedom
ISBN # 1-894331-07-9

Newly Single Man A Celebration of Freedom
ISBN # 1-894331-06-0

Illness - A Small Book of Comfort
ISBN # 1-894331-08-7

The Mourning After - A Small Book of Healing
ISBN # 1-894331-09-5

http://www.wandasthilaire.com

Books to incite impassioned odysseys through life

www.ingramcontent.com/pod-product-compliance
Lightning Source LLC
Chambersburg PA
CBHW071232080526
44587CB00013BA/1581